MEN AT ARMS

Men According to the Anointing, Rigors, and Mandate of Scripture

PAUL AMPONG

This book is dedicated to my wife, Melch, who has modeled for me God's unconditional love, especially when I was the worst version of myself.

With this book, I start to build a literary legacy for my son, Andrsn, to encourage him to fight the good fight, finish the race, and keep the faith.

I love them both to infinity.

PREFACE

The journey to writing this book started with my own personal meditations with the Holy Scriptures. I made a commitment that, as much as possible, I would have a ME Time—that's Majestic Encounter Time—with the Heavenly Father. Much of it involves delving into His Word.

Even before the pandemic, I've already read the Bible a few times. The lockdowns only gave me more time to read and reflect. At first, it was more about the volume of text I read everyday. And then, the Spirit convicted me to dig deeper in my readings—He prompted me to go for quality over quantity. That's when I started taking down learning points and other notes from what I read.

I began to see the interconnectedness of the passages. I have come to believe that this interconnectedness is part of the grand scheme of things that God designed—that all Scriptures lead to Jesus. This made me explore Scripture even more with a greater hunger for the Word.

My readings reminded me of my final year in college wherein I spent a summer in an advanced writing class. Much to my surprise, it was an advanced writing class that did not involve much actual writing. Instead, our activities and assignments primarily revolved around reading books and articles, and watching movies. The professor's principle was "read, read, and read (or watch movies) and then write a little." It got me thinking, "I probably I could 'write a little' now that I have read quite a volume of Scriptures multiple times already."

So, I started writing my thoughts down in my notebook. These notes were more like bullet points or diagrams that illustrate the message revealed to me by the Word of God. Some would be in the form of outlines. When I read and reread my notes, I noticed that they could be used in Bible study settings, in similar ministries, or even in sermons (as I sometimes get invited to speak in UCCP Bradford Church). In fact, I used some sections of a chapter in this book, when it was still in the works, to deliver a sermon in February 2023.

Memories of when I attempted to start a number of ministries flashed in my mind. One of these ministries (which were all in UCCP Bradford Church, Cebu City) was a Bible reading and study group (WeRMS: We Read the Message of Scripture); another was a ministry of creatives in church (Bradford Creatives); another was a Bible study group for a select few men in church (an unnamed ministry). None of them lasted a year.

Looking back, I thought that maybe I was not yet adequately equipped back then. Or maybe, my time had not yet come. Regardless, I figured that writing down my insights would come in handy when I start another ministry again.

Or maybe, I was not called to lead or start ministries. Maybe, I was called to empower others to lead ministries.

Thus, I endeavored to write this book.

The title, *MEN AT ARMS*, is a reference to men-at-arms—medieval knights, usually heavily armed—which have become a symbol of the honor and power of the warrior class. It is also an acronym.

The subtitle, *Men According to the Anointing, Rigors, and Mandate of Scripture*, expounds the acronym and sets the biblical context of the book.

Many of the points presented within the pages of this book were gathered over years of listening to sermons (both on-site and online), attending Bible studies, and reading the Bible.

In the process of proofreading, refining, and editing—while reading the Bible and listening to sermons (mostly from Citichurch, also in Cebu City) in between—I realized that all insights I gained from Scripture reinforce each other. As long as they are centered on the person of Jesus, the learning points perfectly complement each other.

The idea of the Great War was adapted from Focus on the Family's The Truth Project[1]. In this video series, the war between good and evil is referred to as the "Cosmic Battle." I had the privilege of viewing the video curriculum through the efforts of my Christian bosses when I was yet employed as a Senior Planning and Design Engineer.

The writing of this book proceeded with the intention of having a material to use as a Bible study guide for a group of young Christian men. Some sections have been used in a few Bible study sessions already. Parts of these sections have already been edited based on feedbacks and additional insights from those sessions.

---

[1] https://www.focusonthefamily.com/faith/the-truth-project/

Moreover, much of the tone of this book is motivational or inspirational. I believe that the element of motivating readers or the audience is essential in today's generation. Young adults today are said to be the "saddest generation." This book highlights men in the Bible and how they accomplished their "missions" in the hope that they can teach readers valuable lessons in facing challenges in life.

This book is comprised of seven chapters about certain men in the Bible and a concluding section (epilogue) that puts all chapters in perspective. These seven chapters are not all that may be gleaned from the pages of the Bible. In fact, I'm currently reflecting on a few more.

I decided to publish this volume and not wait for me to finish additional chapters for a number of reasons. First, I felt the urgency to share to others the lessons I had learned over the years which I penned in this book. Second, I wanted to learn the process of publication. And third, I am giving space for the Holy Spirit to move and to reveal what the next step would be. This book may be the first volume of an unknown number of books. Only God knows, really.

It should be noted however that this book may be used as a guide for one's personal journey through the Bible regardless of gender.

Although I have personal copies of most of the Bible versions used in this book, using the YouVersion[2] Bible app has made browsing through the different translations a breeze. The app also made writing faster because of its search and copy features.

I would like to specially thank my good friend, Rev. Dr. Van Cliburn Tibus, Dean of Silliman University Divinity School, for indulging me in writing the foreword.

My gratitude to my wife, Melch, and my son, Andrsn—who have always been my inspiration—could not be put into words.

To God be the glory!

Paul Ampong
Guadalupe, Cebu City, Philippines
instagram.com/paulampong.books

---

[2] https://www.youversion.com/

So I sought for a man among them who would make a wall, and stand in the gap before me on behalf of the land, that I should not destroy it; but I found none.

Ezekiel 22:30

FOREWORD

Life is a battle—a struggle between the forces of darkness and the forces of light. The book you read may be full of violent imagery, and you may even be shocked to discover that it is rooted in the Holy Scriptures. Yet, this is a brave testimony of one man's struggle with a rare and life-threatening disease, his finding strength in God's love in Christ, and his gaining insights from biblical stories of warfare and tactics.

Paul acknowledges his imperfections as a Christian. Nevertheless, his experience and knowledge connecting biblical narratives to contemporary events touches every man's dream of achieving ultimate victory.

MEN AT ARMS is a book designed to be read by men. Yet, women can learn a lot about what goes into a man's heart by reading this book.

Most importantly, it talks about a person's struggle with life and the discovery of solace and peace anchored in God's love, manifested through family, friends, and the faith community.

If you are struggling, this book provides practical ways to keep fighting as we are already assured eternal victory in Christ.

Rev. Van Cliburn Tibus, PhD.
Dean
Silliman University Divinity School,
Dumaguete City, Philippines

PROLOGUE

As the title suggests, this book pictures men in the Bible as soldiers—men-at-arms—in the Great War between good and evil, light and darkness, truth and lies. It is often said that the greatest trick that the devil has pulled is convincing people he does not exist. I would say that his second greatest trick is convincing people that the Great War does not exist. It does and its manifestation is already very tangible in the present age with all that is happening in societies all over the world—and we are right in the middle of the fray.

God called men in the Bible to advance His cause and show His love. This book explores different men in the Bible and pictures them as officials or regiments of the Army of God.

The war is real and big. We, as members of the army, are to fight and prevail in little skirmishes—in our workplace, our school, our circle of friends, and even in our family—if we are to win this war. But we have to bear in mind that in every conflict, the enemy is not our fellowmen—our officemates, our classmates, our friends, or our family. The real enemy is the devil.

The war has two sides. On one side are those of us who follow Jesus—the champion of love, life, truth, and good. On the other side is Satan—the champion of hatred, death, lies, and evil.

This book is a call to arms. It hopes to kindle in the hearts of young men to take up the cudgels from those who have gone before us and join the fray. It strives to equip those enlisted in the Army of God with the right weapon—the sword of the Spirit, which is the Word of God.

It is my hope and prayer that this book could make a big impact in the lives of young men growing in the faith of our Lord Jesus Christ.

I believe that men have a special calling. In the following sections, we briefly discuss the anointing, rigors, and mandate of this calling as found in Scripture.

ANOINTING

To anoint is to bestow authority or power on someone; often with oil or similar substances.

In olden times, anointing often involves a personal and a material agent. The best example is the anointing of King David. Samuel was the personal agent to whom God revealed His choice; the oil (most probably olive oil) was the material agent with which the anointing ceremony was done. In those times, prophets and oil were seen to have a strong connection to the Divine.

The passage is found in I Samuel 16. In this Biblical text, we can see that the anointing was (is and always will be) from God. Samuel and the oil were just instruments.

> Then Samuel took the horn of oil and anointed him in the midst of his brothers; and the Spirit of the LORD came upon David from that day forward. So Samuel arose and went to Ramah.
>
> I Samuel 16:13

Notice that after Samuel anointed David, something amazing happened—the Spirit of the LORD came upon David from that day forward. Thus, anointing comes from God through His agents, and it is manifested by the indwelling of the Spirit.

This only slightly changed in the New Testament times.

When Jesus was about to do the ultimate act of love on the cross, He promised those who follow

Him that the Father will send the Helper—none other than the Holy Spirit.

> Nevertheless I tell you the truth. It is to your advantage that I go away; for if I do not go away, the Helper will not come to you; but if I depart, I will send Him to you.

> John 16:7

When we accept Jesus as our Lord and Savior, the Holy Spirit indwells in us. And it is through the Spirit that we receive gifts.

> But the manifestation of the Spirit is given to each one for the profit of all: for to one is given the word of wisdom through the Spirit, to another the word of knowledge through the same Spirit, to another faith by the same Spirit, to another gifts of healings by the same Spirit, to another the working of miracles, to another prophecy, to another discerning of spirits, to another different kinds of tongues, to another the interpretation of tongues.

> I Corinthians 12:7-10

It was through the death and resurrection of Jesus Christ that the Spirit was sent to us. And the Spirit in us gives us gifts—anointing—according to the purpose for which we were sent.

The elements of anointing from ancient times persist—God remains the One who chooses whom to anoint. Our acceptance of the finished work of Christ on the cross serves as the agent, essentially making Jesus the personal agent and His blood the "material" agent. The Holy Spirit within us is the One who manifests the anointing.

RIGORS

When the Israelites were in the wilderness and were on their way to the Promised Land, the rites of worship were instituted. God gave the people strict instructions to follow. It was also during this time that the priesthood of the line of Aaron was established.

In Leviticus 21, we read the strict regulations of conduct for priests. God was very specific. Remember that the tribe of Levi had been set apart for the service of God. But within that tribe, He again set apart a clan. Moses and Aaron were Levites—Levi was their great grandfather. Moses was the first prophet; and Aaron, the first priest. God had set apart the Levites; He further chose the line of Aaron to be priests.

In this chapter of Leviticus, God specified how the priests should live their lives. While not all Levites are priests (in the order of Aaron), the chapter stipulates that not all of Aaron's descendants can be priests. Those with physical defects were disqualified.

> And the LORD spoke to Moses, saying, "Speak to Aaron, saying: 'No man of your descendants in succeeding generations, who has any defect, may approach to offer the bread of his God. For any man who has a defect shall not approach: a man blind or lame, who has a marred face or any limb too long, a man who has a broken foot or broken hand, or is a hunchback or a dwarf, or a man who has a defect in his eye, or eczema or scab, or is a eunuch. No man of the descendants of Aaron the priest, who has a defect, shall come near to offer the offerings made by fire to the LORD. He has a defect; he shall not come near to offer the bread of his God. He may eat the bread of his God, both the most holy and the holy; only he shall not go near the veil or approach the altar, because he has a defect, lest he profane My sanctuaries; for I the LORD sanctify them.' "
>
> Leviticus 21:16-23

Notice how strict the rigors of being a priest were. This, again, changed when Jesus came. The author of the book of Hebrews affirmed that Jesus is the High Priest in the order of Melchizedek.

> And having been perfected, He became the author of eternal salvation to all who obey Him, called by God as High Priest "according to the order of Melchizedek…"
>
> Hebrews 5:9-10

Melchizedek first appeared in the Bible during the time of Abraham. He was both the king of Salem (the old name of Jerusalem) and priest of God Most High. Jesus is King and High Priest.

> Then Melchizedek king of Salem brought out bread and wine; he was the priest of God Most High.
>
> Genesis 14:18

Melchizedek's priesthood was before the institution of the order of Aaron. Jesus, who existed from eternity past with the Father, is also outside the institution of Aaron's priesthood.

> He was in the beginning with God.
>
> John 1:2

And we, the followers of Jesus, are called to be like Him.

> Therefore be imitators of God as dear children. And walk in love, as Christ also has loved us and given Himself for us, an offering and a sacrifice to God for a sweet-smelling aroma.

> Ephesians 5:1-2

After the resurrection of Jesus, the Apostles preached the priesthood of all believers.

> But you are a chosen generation, a royal priesthood, a holy nation, His own special people, that you may proclaim the praises of Him who called you out of darkness into His marvelous light; who once were not a people but are now the people of God, who had not obtained mercy but now have obtained mercy.

> I Peter 2:9-10

Thus, the bar has been raised.

Yes, there are no more physical constraints. But the requirement that priests (i.e., all believers) should be without blemish remains the same. This time, the rigors are spiritual in nature. If the rigors of the priesthood of Aaron were steep, being like Jesus is steeper—we have to strive for perfection.

> "Therefore you shall be perfect, just as your Father in heaven is perfect."
>
> Matthew 5:48

MANDATE

On the sixth day of creation, God spoke and gave man dominion over His creation.

> Then God said, "Let Us make man in Our image, according to Our likeness; let them have dominion over the fish of the sea, over the birds of the air, and over the cattle, over all the earth and over every creeping thing that creeps on the earth."
>
> Genesis 1:26

Thus, God relegated dominion over to humans—specifically to Adam, the first man. This was His mandate to man. And God never goes against His words.

This is evident in how God acted throughout history as recorded in the Bible. Our all-powerful God always uses human instruments to do His will. He directed Noah to build the ark so that mankind and all animals would be saved from the flood; He used Ezekiel to speak life into the dry bones in the desert; and, of course, He sent His one and only son, Jesus—fully human and fully divine—to save us all from our sins.

Thus, as we begin our journey across the Bible through this book, we will see that at every turn, God would choose a man to do His will. In this volume, seven men or groups of men are featured as officers or units of the Army of God.

SCRIPTURE

Again, our ultimate weapon in this war is the Holy Bible.

> For the word of God is living and powerful, and sharper than any two-edged sword, piercing even to the division of soul and spirit, and of joints and marrow, and is a discerner of the thoughts and intents of the heart.
>
> Hebrews 4:12

The reader will find that all points presented in this book are backed by the Word of God. Scriptures that support any argument herein are quoted with the specific versions of the Bible used.

In the succeeding chapters, we will see how God would *anoint* men to achieve His purpose. These men, even if they lived in Old Testament times, would give us glimpses of Jesus' nature and character—giving us pointers on how to navigate through the *rigors* of being Christ-like. And we will discover that God upholds his *mandate* to man throughout history and in our personal journey with Him. All these in accordance to what is found in *Scripture*.

Who is the one who is victorious and overcomes the world? It is the one who believes and recognizes the fact that Jesus is the Son of God.
1 John 5:5 AMP

THE VANGUARD

EXODUS 3

A vanguard is the frontline of an advancing army.

We now live in a world with much less wars than there were in ancient times. Not counting the Great War, wars in modern times still exist but they now come in much watered down forms—sports. Technically, in any sporting event, two teams compete—or fight—against each other until one betters and beats the other.

One sport that is beloved the world over, especially in the Philippines, is basketball. Competing teams in a basketball game usually have a roster of twelve players but only five can play at a time. And the game starts with each team fielding in its five top players, known as the starting lineup or the first five.

The starting lineup is the vanguard of the team.

Moses is regarded as the first leader of the people of Israel. He was at the vanguard of an advancing nation.

We read in Exodus 3 the account of how Moses was called by God—how God manifested Himself through a burning bush in Mount Horeb and gave His marching orders to Moses.

THE ENCOUNTER

We, who grew up in Sunday school, have always seen Moses as an extraordinary man—a great leader of the Israelites who led them out of the land of bondage in Egypt to the Promised Land. But it was not always so.

In earlier chapters, we learn that Moses was just like any other Israelite baby born in Egypt. What set him apart was the fact that he was delivered from the hands of Pharaoh and was adopted into the royal family according to God's intricate plan. But that privilege did not last long.

When he became a grown man, he fled from Egypt because of an incident where he killed an Egyptian slave driver. He sought refuge in the wilderness for his life and eventually found himself in the house of Jethro, the priest of Midian.

The account in Exodus 3, which was about 40 years after he left Egypt, opens with a very ordinary scene: Moses tending the flock of his father-in-law in Mt. Horeb, which is another name for Mt. Sinai.

Then, there was the call—the burning bush experience. What made an ordinary day an extraordinary encounter was how Moses responded.

> And the Angel of the LORD appeared to him in a flame of fire from the midst of the bush. So **he looked**, and behold, the bush was burning with fire, but the bush was not consumed.
>
> Exodus 3:2; emphasis mine

The burning bush may have been at a little distance from him; he may have heard the call and saw part of the spectacle. But the call necessitated some level of action from Moses—he had to get a closer look and listen closely to the call.

It was here that God made Himself known to Moses. It was here that God gave Moses His marching orders.

> Moreover He said, "**I am the God of your father**—the God of Abraham, the God of

Isaac, and the God of Jacob." And Moses hid his face, for he was afraid to look upon God.

And the LORD said: "**I have surely seen** the oppression of My people who are in Egypt, and **have heard** their cry because of their taskmasters, for I know their sorrows. So **I have come down** to deliver them out of the hand of the Egyptians, and to bring them up from that land to a good and large land, to a land flowing with milk and honey, to the place of the Canaanites and the Hittites and the Amorites and the Perizzites and the Hivites and the Jebusites. Now therefore, behold, **the cry of the children of Israel has come to Me**, and **I have also seen** the oppression with which the Egyptians oppress them. Come now, therefore, and I will send you to Pharaoh that you may bring My people, the children of Israel, out of Egypt."

Exodus 3:6-10; emphases mine

As the text above suggests, any ordinary day can become an extraordinary encounter. We just have to know "where to look" to see amazing things unfold before our eyes. But that, again, requires an effort from our end. If Moses did not check out that great spectacle we now call the burning bush experience, he would never have become God's instrument.

Moses' case may have been different. There was a miraculous phenomenon right before him. It was more than enough to pique his interest. But it required him to be brave.

And this is where we are all on level ground. We may not have a spectacle of the same magnitude as the burning bush. All we may encounter are mundane things of everyday life. But seeing the miracle in these simple things requires the same level of bravery.

Know who God is

When God revealed Himself to Moses, He first introduced who He was, saying, "I am the God of your father—the God of Abraham, the God of Isaac, and the God of Jacob." For those who have grown in faith and wisdom, this would have been enough to allay all doubts and fears.

> "Be still, and **know** that I am God! I am exalted among the nations, I am exalted in the earth."
>
> Psalms 46:10; emphasis mine

Moses apparently had all sorts of doubts and fears. We are not any different. This is especially true if we don't understand things around us.

Every time we make decisions, it is an opportunity for an extraordinary encounter. If we intimately know who God is, our decisions, whether big or small, will be guided with divine wisdom. Knowing who He is means knowing what He wants. Knowing what He wants means knowing what He wants for us. All we have to do next is to align our decisions with who He is and what He wants for us.

See what He has done

Many times, even if we know who God is, we are blinded by the many troubles around us. In moments like this, God, like in Moses' burning bush experience, reminds us of what He has done.

Many of us may be in a hard situation right now, but surely we can recall mountaintop experiences in the past where we have clearly seen His handiwork.

> I will remember the works of the LORD;
> Surely I will remember Your wonders of old.
>
> Psalms 77:11

Or, we just have to read our Bibles. The Holy Scripture is filled with narratives of what God has done for His people.

In the Exodus 3 text, after He introduced Himself to Moses, God said, "I *have* surely *seen*... ...and *have heard*... So I *have come down*...".

Notice that the text uses the present perfect tense of the verbs. According to thesaurus.com, "One of the main reasons we use the present perfect tense is to indicate that a state or action that happened or started in the past has some connection to the present and future."

This means that God saw, heard and came down sometime in the past and was about to do something when He appeared to Moses in the burning bush. Not only that the statements imply that God still sees and hears in the present, they also say that He has a plan for the future.

> "For I know the plans I have for you," declares the LORD, "plans to prosper you and not to harm you, plans to give you hope and a future."
>
> Jeremiah 29:11 NIV

We all live in the present. And the present is the pivot point between the past and the future. God calls us to be His instrument to achieve His plans in the present.

Do His will

The extraordinary will only become more extraordinary if we dare to answer the call and be God's instrument for His plans. Moses, for his part, tried to wiggle his way out of God's call.

Then Moses answered and said, "But suppose they will not believe me or listen to my voice; suppose they say, 'The LORD has not appeared to you.' "

Exodus 4:1

God showed him signs to address his apprehensions, yet he still had more excuses.

Then Moses said to the LORD, "O my Lord, I am not eloquent, neither before nor since You have spoken to Your servant; but I am slow of speech and slow of tongue."

Exodus 4:10

In many ways, we are not any different.

Moses became a major player in the history of Israel because he said "Yes" to the call despite many excuses. Due to his numerous excuses, Moses is generally not viewed as the role model in answering the call of God. The prophet Isaiah did a much better job in this regard.

Also I heard the voice of the Lord, saying: "Whom shall I send, And who will go for Us?" Then I said, "**Here am I! Send me.**"

Isaiah 6:8; emphasis mine

The preceding passage is from the chapter where Isaiah had a vision of the LORD on the throne and it was during this moment when he was called to be a prophet.

Moses may not have responded as Isaiah did centuries later, but he answered the call by allowing himself to be an instrument of God—by doing His will.

In New Testament times, Jesus told the people the Parable of the Two Sons.

> "But what do you think? A man had two sons, and he came to the first and said, 'Son, go, work today in my vineyard.' He answered and said, 'I will not,' but afterward he regretted it and went. Then he came to the second and said likewise. And he answered and said, 'I go, sir,' but he did not go. Which of the two did the will of his father?" They said to Him, "The first." Jesus said to them, "Assuredly, I say to you that tax collectors and harlots enter the kingdom of God before you..."
>
> Matthew 21:28-31

God's words are powerful, true, and eternal. Whatever He says becomes reality—He spoke the universe into being. But though we were created in the image of God, human words are not as steadfast as His. God understands this. For us humans, "Actions speak louder than words." That is why in the parable, the one who did the action was the one who did the father's will.

Doing God's will is answering His call.

THE MISSION

Moses encountered God in Mt. Horeb. There he experienced what it is like to be in the presence of God. It was there that God gave Moses his mission. But what was the mission?

The purpose

To answer that question, we must first learn the purpose of God. In Exodus 3:8, we read, "So I have come down to deliver them out of the hand of the Egyptians, and to bring them up from that land to a good and large land..."

This is God's purpose for coming down—to do what He desires to do, to fulfill the promise He first gave to Abraham. Remember that Abraham's inheritance was entirely by God's grace. He did not earn it. God speaks his promises out of his amazing grace and He does not go back on His words.

Now the LORD had said to Abram[3]: "Get out of your country, From your family And from your father's house, To a land that I will show you."

Then the LORD appeared to Abram and said, "To your descendants I will give this land." And there he built an altar to the Lord, who had appeared to him.

Genesis 12:1, 7

Back to the question: What was Moses' mission?

Verse 10 of Exodus 3 says, "... I will send you to... bring My people... out of Egypt." His mission was to be God's instrument to fulfill His purpose. His mission was to align his life's purpose to God's.

And so it is for us.

We are God's agents of change, of deliverance, of blessings. Only He can bring about change to the lives of people and in the world. Only He can deliver us from whatever dire circumstances we are in. Only He can bless us beyond measure. But He needs a channel. Our mission, just like Moses', is to be that channel. Again, recall that God has already

---

[3] Abram was Abraham's original name before God changed it

relegated dominion of the entire world to the hands of humankind—to Adam—in the Garden of Eden.

If we refuse to be God's channel—God's agent—we will miss the chance to be of service to Him. Surely, He will fulfill His purpose through someone else or some other means. But if you are in the position to do the mission, by all means do it. Remember what Mordecai told Esther when she was still undecided to help her fellowmen?

> For if you remain completely silent at this time, relief and deliverance will arise for the Jews from another place, but you and your father's house will perish. Yet who knows whether you have come to the kingdom for such a time as this?
>
> Esther 4:14

It's very human to fear that if we embark on a mission to do God's purpose, we might fail—we might make a joke out of ourselves. But we should not worry about that. The Apostle Paul told the early Christians in Rome:

> And we know that all things work together for good to those who love God, to those who are the called according to His purpose.
>
> Romans 8:28

But then, how do we know that what we are doing is according to His purpose?

The sign

Asking for signs is also very human. The Old Testament judge Gideon is infamous for asking one sign too many. When he was called to deliver the Israelites from the hands of the Midianites, he asked God for signs.

> So Gideon said to God, "If You will save Israel by my hand as You have said— look, I shall put a fleece of wool on the threshing floor; if there is dew on the fleece only, and it is dry on all the ground, then I shall know that You will save Israel by my hand, as You have said."
>
> Judges 6:36-37

Gideon did not stop there. When God gave him the sign, he asked for another on the next day—a reverse of what he had first asked. Even right before they attacked the enemy camp, God continued to assure him of victory—He gave him another sign.

We, humans, crave for assurance. God is the Great Assurer.

Back to Exodus 3: God assured Moses that there will be a sign that indeed it was He who sent him.

So He said, "I will certainly be with you. And this shall be a sign to you that I have sent you: When you have brought the people out of Egypt, you shall serve God on this mountain."

Exodus 3:12

In the burning bush experience, Moses had a personal encounter with God and he worshipped Him. God wanted the people to have the same experience, the same encounter, on the same place.

If we are able to make others see God's goodness and greatness in our lives—so much so that they encounter Him in their own lives as well—then we can say that we are fulfilling our mission of serving His purpose.

When we say "Yes!" to the call, we will surely have our own mountaintop experiences. It is part of our mission to allow others to have the same experience: worshipping God where He meets us.

I have experienced God's grace and greatness in many ways but the most pronounced of all was His healing. Those who know me would attest that I have battled against a critical illness since I was three years old. It never manifested itself again since then until I was 33 years old.

In 2017, I had a series of stroke-like attacks. These attacks led to several visits to the hospital where various tests were done on me. The diagnosis was Multiple Sclerosis—a critical illness that is rare in tropical countries like the Philippines. Modern science has not fully understood the illness—its causes and treatment—yet. The only available medication is not for cure but for reduction of future attacks. I decided not to take it partly because it was so expensive.

In the back of my mind, I was hoping for God's healing power. I did not get healed the way I expected to be healed. But His presence in my life throughout my journey cannot be denied. For one, my Multiple Sclerosis is very mild compared to others'. That is a blessing in itself.

I did not see it that way at first. Instead, I succumbed to depression. Although I was not clinically diagnosed, I showed several of its symptoms. That was when God's presence became more tangible.

Looking back, I was the worst version of myself. But God's love was very evident. He surrounded me with people who manifested His love for me—my wife, Melch, most especially.

God also provided financially. Family and friends from all over the world shared portions of their resources to us. God had also provided us the wisdom to create a separate fund for medical emergencies. All these God provided so that we didn't have to start from scratch all over again financially.

I hope no one will go through medical issues like I did, but I wish everyone will experience the healing power of God, in the name of Jesus and by the power of the Holy Spirit, and be able to worship Him regardless of circumstances.

God's grace is so amazing that He has sustained me and my family through all these years. I love to tell my story to people so that they will know that God is still doing miracles.

Thus, I boldly declare: I am living a miracle; I am a living miracle!

The journey

Notice also that the mountaintop experience of Moses, and later of the Israelites, happened before they arrived at their destination. This simply means that worship is not to be in the destination. It's to be part of the journey.

Yes, God promised to bring them to a good and large land—a land flowing with milk and honey. But the Promised Land was not where He would meet them. In fact, He was with them in their journey through the wilderness from the beginning. And He would come down from time to time to meet them and even meet their needs.

The people encountered God throughout the journey. But the journey was not without bumps and detours. Whenever they encountered something big, God would only prove to them that He was bigger.

While our main mission may be to bring people to a "place" that God promised, we should not miss out on encounters with Him in our daily walk.

THE WEAPON

God does not send someone into the battlefield without a weapon. Our mistake oftentimes is to look far to find that weapon.

When Moses started making excuses to not heed the call, God simply asked him, "What is that in your hand?"

> So the LORD said to him, "What is that in your hand?" He said, "A rod."

> Exodus 4:2

Yes, Scripture is our ultimate weapon in this war. But God has also equipped us with talents and skills (see I Corinthians 12:7-11) that are unique to each one of us—these are what we have in our hands.

We all have different gifts from the Spirit. As an army, with Jesus as the Commander-in-Chief, we are an unstoppable force.

When David volunteered to fight the giant Goliath, Saul wanted him to wear his armor and sword to battle. But they were too big and heavy for the young boy.

> David fastened his sword to his armor and tried to walk, for he had not tested them. And David said to Saul, "I cannot walk with these, for I have not tested them." So David took them off.
>
> I Samuel 17:39

Many times in our life—in ministry or in the workplace—some people would impose their ways, their methods, their styles on us. And we can't blame them. Their ways have worked for them in the past. To them, they are only helping us out— which is good. But God uniquely created all of us. He has equipped us with innate qualities that fit our ways to do His purpose.

So what did David do?

Then he took his **staff** *in his hand*; and he chose for himself five smooth stones from the brook, and put them in a **shepherd's bag**, *in a pouch which he had*, and his **sling** was *in his hand*. And he drew near to the Philistine.

I Samuel 17:40; emphases mine

David did not wander far from who and what he was—a shepherd. He didn't use Saul's belongings. He used the instruments of a shepherd as weapons of war. He was bold enough to go into battle without actual weapons.

His conviction stemmed from a deep understanding in his heart that God was on his side. He boldly declared that he will defeat the giant so "All the earth may know that there is a God in Israel" (v. 46). He then further declared:

Then all this assembly shall know that the LORD does not save with sword and spear; for the battle is the LORD's, and He will give you into our hands.

I Samuel 17:47

The battle belongs to the LORD! We can only boldly declare this if we know Him intimately.

Like David, Moses also had a rod—the tool of a shepherd. God would use his rod to work wonders.

But Moses made more excuses. So, God said He would send Aaron, his brother, to be his mouthpiece. Thus, God augments our individual strengths with the strengths of our comrades. Again, we are an army. And we have our brothers-at-arms with us.

> **Two are better than one**, Because they have a good reward for their labor. For if they fall, one will lift up his companion. But woe to him who is alone when he falls, For he has no one to help him up. Again, if two lie down together, they will keep warm; But how can one be warm alone? Though one may be overpowered by another, two can withstand him. And **a threefold cord is not quickly broken**.
>
> Ecclesiastes 4:9-12; emphases mine

During His ministry on earth, Jesus even sent his disciples by pairs.

> After these things the Lord appointed seventy others also, and sent them **two by two** before His face into every city and place where He Himself was about to go.
>
> Luke 10:1; emphasis mine

Jesus Himself acknowledged the power of brotherhood—of having someone on your side, especially in doing His work. We see this repeated over and over again in the Bible.

It's a number's game. King Solomon, in Ecclesiastes, mentioned that a cord with three strands is not easily broken. And for any one-on-one personal relationship, Jesus is the third person that makes the bond stronger.

God never sends us out to battle empty handed.

Let us all be ready to have an encounter with God. It can happen everyday—whenever we spend some quality time with Him. We only have to be keen to His still small voice. It may take some practice but when we hear His call, let us align our priorities with His purpose. And let's not look far. The weapon we need to accomplish His call may be right under our noses.

THE WARRIOR

I SAMUEL 17

A warrior is one who goes into the thick of battle regardless of rank.

Many ancient societies operated on a caste system. One of the most interesting of these societies was ancient Japan. In this society, the warrior class was put on a pedestal. The samurais were pledged to protect their masters even if it cost them their lives. They embodied honor and loyalty. And in the time of feudal wars, their ability to protect their lords was highly valued. They were even willing to take their own lives if they were unable to do their duty.

Such is the heart of a warrior.

David was the greatest king in the history of Israel. Before he became king, he was a shepherd boy. But all the while, he was a warrior. He was a warrior even while he was a shepherd; he was a warrior even after he was crowned king.

The event that highlighted his role as a warrior is the all-time favorite Bible narrative of him fighting Goliath. The narrative is found in I Samuel 17—which is probably my favorite Chapter in the Old Testament as I have found myself reading it over and over again and learning new lessons every time.

THE BRIEF

Many are familiar with the narrative of David fighting Goliath, but not so many people know the backstory. David's story actually began when he was anointed by the prophet Samuel to be the next king of Israel. One day God spoke to Samuel, revealing that He had chosen for Himself the next king, for He had rejected Saul.

> Now the LORD said to Samuel, "How long will you mourn for Saul, seeing I have rejected him from reigning over Israel? Fill your horn with oil, and go; I am sending you to Jesse the Bethlehemite. For I have provided Myself a king among his sons."
>
> I Samuel 16:1

The unlikely hero

God's instruction was for Samuel to go to Bethlehem to see a man named Jesse, as He had chosen one of Jesse's sons for a divine purpose. So,

Samuel went to Bethlehem and invited Jesse and his sons, and, most likely, some other people to offer a sacrifice to the Living God. Then, he revealed his real objective—which was to anoint the next king of Israel from one of Jesse's sons.

Jesse presented each of his sons before Samuel, seeking to determine which one of them was the chosen one. The screening started with the eldest, Eliab; then the second son, Abinadab; and then the third son, Shammah. This went on for four more sons of Jesse. But after Jesse presented his seven sons, Samuel said God had not chosen any of them.

Samuel asked Jesse if he still had another son and Jesse said (in I Samuel 16:11), "Yes, there's one more —the youngest one and he's out tending the sheep." Samuel asked for the young boy to be fetched, for they would not proceed without him.

David must have been confused when he arrived to see his father, his brothers, the prophet Samuel, and many of their neighbors in the crowd. All the people around may have had their eyes fixed on David.

God spoke to Samuel, saying, "Arise, anoint him; for this is the one." (I Samuel 16:12)

Being the last of eight brothers, especially in the Jewish culture, David was the unlikely hero of the day. The prophet navigated through seven of his older brothers to reach him.

Many times in our lives, even in ministry, we feel that we are the most unlikely person for the job. And it is but human to feel we are unworthy for a higher calling because we don't have the skills or experience. We seem to forget that many times in history God has chosen the unlikeliest person in the unlikeliest situation to do amazing things. The world might call it luck; wiser people may call it fate or destiny. But I call it God's unfathomable wisdom.

This reminds me of another war narrative in the Bible. During the time of the Divided Kingdom, Jehoshaphat, king of Judah, joined forces with Ahab, king of Israel, to face the enemy—the king of Syria. Syria is geographically nearer to Samaria, the capital of the Northern Kingdom of Israel, than to Jerusalem, the capital of the Southern Kingdom of Judah. Syria and Israel were periodically at war with each other. The king of Israel disguised himself so that the enemy would not recognize him in the battlefield. The plan worked. The enemy couldn't find Ahab in the battlefield. But a random guy, an archer, arbitrarily releases an arrow. The arrow found its way between the plates of the armor of the king of Israel.

Now a certain man drew a bow at random, and struck the king of Israel between the joints of his armor. So he said to the driver of his chariot, "Turn around and take me out of the battle, for I am wounded."

I Kings 22:34

What were the odds?

Some things may seem unlikely to happen by the rules of probability or by the natural laws of the universe. But the world almost always forgets that the universe is God's and that He can move freely regardless of geographic or temporal constraints. David may have been the most unlikely hero of the day but he was the one chosen by God. For God operates on a level of His own—beyond probability and the natural laws of the universe.

God deemed David to be the most qualified because of the matter of his heart.

The heart of the matter

I have come to believe that the heart of the matter is the matter of the heart.

When Jesse asked his eldest son to see Samuel, Eliab must have looked physically superior to most men. Naturally, Samuel almost instantly thought that Eliab, the eldest, was the chosen one.

But the LORD said to Samuel, "Do not look at his appearance or at his physical stature, because I have refused him. For the LORD does not see as man sees; for man looks at the outward appearance, but the LORD looks at the heart."

I Samuel 16:7

God indeed operates differently. David would go down in history as the man after God's own heart.

That's something big.

The physical heart is one of the most amazing organs in the human body. It is made of special muscles that are designed to continuously pump over a person's lifetime. Other muscles would need rest and relaxation from time to time in order to grow, develop, and regain strength—but not the heart. These cardiac muscles were tuned to beat at a design speed to give all parts of the body the right amount of blood and oxygen. Without the heart, the entire human body shuts down.

In the Bible, the word "heart" does not refer to the physical heart. It refers to the core of the person's thoughts—the will and the mind combined. This is evident in how authors of the Bible write and how different versions of the Bible translate certain passages.

For instance, when Jesus was asked which one was the first (and greatest) commandment, He quoted the shema[4].

> And Jesus answered him, The first of all the commandments is, Hear, O Israel; The Lord our God is one Lord: and thou shalt love the Lord thy God with all thy **heart**, and with all thy soul, and with all thy **mind**, and with all thy strength: this is the first commandment.
>
> Mark 12:29-30 KJV; emphases mine

Jesus, in this passage, was referring to an Old Testament scripture. Interestingly, Jesus dissected the original text of "heart" into "heart and mind."

> "Hear, O Israel: The LORD our God is one LORD: and thou shalt love the LORD thy God with all thine **heart**, and with all thy soul, and with all thy might."
>
> Deuteronomy 6:4-5 KJV; emphasis mine

The Gospel of Mark is wildly accepted as the earliest book of the New Testament. The King

---

4 Shema is a Hebrew word that means "hear." This is the first word in Deuteronomy 6:4. The word also refers to this and following verses and to the prayer of which these verses are a part.

James Version (KJV) is also regarded as one of the earliest English translations. A newer translation of the Bible, the Amplified Bible (AMP), also emphasizes heart and mind.

> "Hear, O Israel! The LORD is our God, the LORD is one [the only God]! You shall love the LORD your God with all your **heart and mind** and with all your soul and with all your strength [your entire being]."
>
> Deuteronomy 6:4-5 AMP; emphasis mine

Over time, the meaning of the word "heart" would come to mean the core[5] of a system or an organization. Without its heart, the human body, an organization, or a system, simply does not work.

And God, who designed the human body, recognizes the importance of the heart. King Solomon, who wrote most of the Proverbs, urged us to guard our hearts.

> Guard your heart above all else, for it determines the course of your life.
>
> Proverbs 4:23 NLT

---

[5] Google says that the word "core" is of unknown origin. But I think it is derived from the Spanish word "corazon" which means heart. Coincidentally, my mother's name is Corazon.

It was indeed so in the case of David. Because God knew the "quality" of his heart, his heart determined the course of his life.

The prelude

We have already established that David would become the next king of Israel. But he wouldn't be for the next few decades. Before he was king, he was first a son to his father. That was the first role he played here on earth. And so it is for us.

However, many us forget *that*, especially as we grow older and gain more knowledge and experiences. We think of ourselves better than the people around us. We forget to play that very first role—as children to our parents.

> Honor your father and your mother, that your days may be long upon the land which the LORD your God is giving you.
>
> Exodus 20:12

This is very important because one of the Ten Commandments specifically commands all children to honor their father and mother. The Apostle Paul emphasized this in his letter to the Ephesians.

> Children, obey your parents in the Lord, for this is right. "Honor your father and mother," which is the first commandment with

promise: "that it may be well with you and you may live long on the earth."

Ephesians 6:1-3

And how was David as a son? The least we can say about him is that he was obedient to his father. Recall that when Samuel came to their town to look for the new king, his father left him out. He was out in the field while his seven brothers lined up to meet the prophet. But that did not deter David from being obedient. In fact, the very reason why he was out in the field was because he was tending his father's flock. He was doing what his father had asked him to do.

And this leads us to the second role that David played before he was king. He was a shepherd.

When I was growing up, my dad kept at least a pair of goats and a cow. It was my responsibility to take the animals out of the shed early in the morning so that they could graze in some grassy patch of land in town. After spending the day at school, I would bring the animals back to the shed. That was one of my chores as a kid. I never really knew what happened to those animals. I guess my dad sold them for their meat.

But in the case of David, it was on a different level. As a shepherd he spent hours within a day to tend the flock. Remember that in the ancient Hebrew culture, the sheep was a big part of their day to day life. The wool was used as clothing material, while the meat and the fats were utilized in their worship rites. Taking care of the sheep meant that David was taking care of the needs of his family.

Protecting the flock was another thing entirely. Tending the flock required him to be in the field where wild animals would come and try to devour the sheep. As recorded in the Bible, David would fight lions and bears that attack the sheep that were under his care.

David's time as a shepherd also played a major role in his daily walk with God. It is most likely that during his time tending the flock that he penned the most famous of all psalms—Psalm 23.

> The LORD is my shepherd;
>
> I shall not want.
>
> He makes me to lie down in green pastures;
>
> He leads me beside the still waters.
>
> He restores my soul;
>
> He leads me in the paths of righteousness
>
> For His name's sake.
>
> Yea, though I walk through the valley of the shadow of death,

I will fear no evil;

For You are with me;

Your rod and Your staff, they comfort me.

You prepare a table before me in the
presence of my enemies;

You anoint my head with oil;

My cup runs over.

Surely goodness and mercy shall follow me

All the days of my life;

And I will dwell in the house of the LORD

Forever.

Psalms 23:1-6

So how was David as a shepherd? He was a good
one to say the least.

David did well in his first roles—as a son and as a
shepherd.

*This reminds me of the time when I was still
teaching in one of the universities here in the city.
One typical school day, a student approached me,
seeking permission to skip the next class. This was
during the time in my teaching years when I didn't
check attendance. So, it really didn't matter whether
or not a certain student would miss a class.*

Attendance didn't factor into how I graded students at that time.

However, he proceeded to explain that he intended to miss the next class to engage in some campaigning activities for the upcoming student government election. He was running for a position in the student council.

His reasoning kind of triggered something in me.

I told him something to the effect of: "You know that I don't check attendance—it's not part of how I grade your performance in class. I will hold you responsible to cope up with whatever lesson you would miss. It's good that you are training yourself up to be a student leader, but never forget that you are a student first—that's your responsibility and duty as a son to your parents. Being a leader only comes second."

David never neglected his first roles—as a son and as a shepherd. We read in I Samuel 17 that David continued to be an obedient son and a good shepherd even after he was anointed king.

> But David occasionally went and returned from Saul to feed his father's sheep at Bethlehem.

Then Jesse said to his son David, "Take now for your brothers an ephah of this dried grain and these ten loaves, and run to your brothers at the camp. And carry these ten cheeses to the captain of their thousand, and see how your brothers fare, and bring back news of them."

So David **rose early** in the morning, **left the sheep with a keeper**, and took the things and went as Jesse had commanded him. And he came to the camp as the army was going out to the fight and shouting for the battle. And David **left his supplies in the hand of the supply keeper**, ran to the army, and came and greeted his brothers.

I Samuel 17:15, 17-18, 20, 22; emphases mine

If it were me—having learned that I would be the next king of an entire nation (which included my family and friends), I would ditch my first roles. I would be waving a banner all over the people that says "I will be king!"

Again, David remained an obedient son and a good shepherd. In the passage above, after receiving his father's command, David did not complain or object. Instead, he rose early the next morning.

This brings me to a time in high school when my grandfather—the late Aureo Nayve Ampong, a righteous man I deeply admire—served as a member of the Board of Trustees at our school. One day, the school requested me to personally deliver a letter to him—an invitation to an upcoming board meeting. I don't recall much what happened next. It's possible I forgot to give him the letter or, perhaps, I procrastinated. I delayed handing him the letter so much that the meeting happened without his presence.

Delayed obedience almost always becomes disobedience. David obeyed his father without delay.

Before he left, David made sure that someone would watch the sheep while he was away. He left someone in charge. The flock of his father was the responsibility of David. Watching over it was his duty. He wouldn't let his absence compromise its welfare. That's a mark of a good shepherd!

He also left the supplies he brought for the army in the hand of the supply keeper.

He was responsible as a shepherd and as a son. Little did David know that being an obedient son and a good shepherd would set him up to be at the forefront of the greatest battle in history. This would catapult David's role as a warrior.

THE STANDOFF

When David arrived at the scene, he may have expected to see intense fighting, but there was none. Instead, there was a standoff. The Philistines were lined up on one hill, the Israelites on another. A valley was between the two armies. It was there that David would hear the taunting and mocking of the giant. As it appears, it had been the same for 40 days already.

> Then he stood and cried out to the armies of Israel, and said to them, "Why have you come out to line up for battle? Am I not a Philistine, and you the servants of Saul? Choose a man for yourselves, and let him come down to me. If he is able to fight with me and kill me, then we will be your servants. But if I prevail against him and kill him, then you shall be our servants and serve us." And the Philistine said, "I defy the armies of Israel this day; give me a man, that we may fight together."
>
> I Samuel 17:8-10

Do not let the enemy define the terms

There are several historical battles and wars recorded in the Bible, but this is the only one where a one-on-one fight decides the outcome. Have in mind that this event happened after the time of the

Judges. The time of the kings began about 360 years after the people entered the land. The army was composed of 14th—give or take—generation Israelites since they entered the Promised Land. The Philistines on the other hand were from a few city-states near the Mediterranean. The Israelites could have easily outnumbered the Philistines.

What caused the standoff was fear. The Israelites feared the enemy because they had let him define the terms of battle. The Israelites had regretfully forgotten that some generations earlier, God, through Moses, made a powerful statement:

> The LORD will fight for you, and you shall hold your peace.
>
> Exodus 14:14

They have forgotten that God was and always has been with them. They had let their fear of the giant get in the way of God's peace.

Many times in our life, we fight losing battles because we let the enemy define the terms. We play his game. We fight in his element.

I remember the much awaited fight between Manny Pacquiao and Floyd Mayweather, Jr. That fight was so big that our group in the couples ministry gathered in one place to watch the fight live on television. Our host even bought a new and bigger screen for that event.

Many people, especially Filipinos, expected Manny to dominate the fight because he had the strength and the speed. But all our hopes went down the drain. Throughout the fight, Mayweather, Jr. dictated the pace.

Yes, Manny had the power in his left hand and the speed to dominate his opponents in most of his fights. He was, in essence, a brawler. Almost always, when the opponent is forced to brawl with him— when he sets the pace—he would win.

But in the Floyd Mayweather, Jr. fight, Manny was forced to box—the forte of tacticians like Mayweather, Jr. Instead of dictating the pace, Manny was forced to fight in the opponent's pace. That to me was the reason he lost the fight.

Whatever giant you are facing right now, don't let it define the terms. Focus on God's promises—on His Word. Our God is bigger than any giant. The moment you let the enemy define the terms, the battle is already lost.

Do not fear to step up

It was fear that gripped the Israelite army to not take action against the giant. It was fear that crippled them—that made them tremble in the face of the enemy. Fear is the weapon of the enemy.

When David learned that there was no one brave enough to face the giant, he asked around (I Samuel 17:29) "Isn't there a cause in this battle?" He wanted the army to remember their cause—the higher reason why they were lined up for battle.

David heard the giant insulting his nation and insulting the One True God. He couldn't stand it. Much more, he couldn't stand the inaction of his people against the enemy.

In our endeavors in life, the best way to surmount any challenge that we face is to know our cause— the biggest reason we do what we do; our biggest "why." If we find that, then we can find the strength to overcome fear, and step up and go into battle, even against a giant.

On March 11, 2011 a devastating earthquake struck Japan off its northeastern coast which generated a tsunami. The catastrophe was compounded when a series of accidents occurred in a nuclear power plant in Fukushima which resulted in the meltdown of the nuclear cores.

The damage was great. It would have been greater if not for a number of heroes who stepped up despite the risk of contamination. They boldly went to ground zero in order to put out fires and flood the heated cores with seawater.

The world would come to know them as the Fukushima 50 (though their actual number was greater). Many never revealed their identities. None of them considered themselves heroes—to themselves, they were just people with a deep sense of duty. The cause of protecting their fellowmen was enough for them to make such sacrificial acts.

David just would not accept the terms of the giant—that if he wins the battle, David and all of his people will become the slaves of the Philistines. He refused the idea of defeat. The cause of protecting his family, friends, and the entire Israelite nation—God's chosen people—from the threats of the enemy was so big that he found the strength to step up.

Do not consider the giant as the destination

Retracing the events in the life of David, we see that he wouldn't have had the opportunity to be an instrument of God had he acted differently. But the giant was merely a hurdle. The battle was not his destiny; he was destined to be king. The giant was just an obstacle he needed to overcome before he could reach his preordained place in history.

We all have big dreams. That's normal. In fact, it was God who put them in our hearts.

He has made everything beautiful in its time. Also **He has put eternity in their hearts**, except that no one can find out the work that God does from beginning to end.

Ecclesiastes 3:11; emphasis mine

Reviewees, graduates who are reviewing in preparation for the board examinations to get their professional licenses from the Professional Regulatory Board (PRC), hold a special place in my heart. Having taken (and passed) three different board exams myself, I think I know what most of them feel as the big day draws near. Whenever I meet any of them, I would tell them what I told myself many years back: the exam is not the destination; it's just an obstacle.

For these reviewees, the upcoming exam is a giant. I firmly believe that any anxiety caused by such a giant could be avoided if only they see the truth that the exam is not the destination; it is but a hurdle. The finish line is beyond the hurdle.

We may be a long way from our big dream right now. We may be facing giants right now. Don't forget that they are just obstacles. God has a higher calling for us. We may not know what it is now, but let us make the most of what we have now and don't miss the chance of making a breakthrough towards that higher call. Remember that God has also promised to see you through it.

> I am confident of this, that the one who began a good work among you will bring it to completion by the day of Jesus Christ.

> Philippians 1:6 NRSV

David fully believed in God's words that he would be the next king. If he did not fight the giant, God may have used someone else to make good of what He said. But then, David would have missed the chance to be God's instrument and to win the heart of the people. Remember, especially during that time of wars and conquests, people almost always rally behind a strong leader. David showed that, with God's help, he was a strong leader. And in the process, he gave glory to God.

THE ARMOR

Much can be said about David's weapon which we have previously discussed (but not exhaustively). In *The Vanguard*, we briefly mentioned that the word of God is our ultimate weapon in this war. We also discussed that God has gifted us with unique gifts which we can use where He has called us to be.

But according to the Apostle Paul in his letter to the Ephesians, the weapon is only part of the whole armor of God. Paul spoke about six pieces of the whole armor—only one of those is a weapon. The rest are protective gears designed to protect the warrior from the attacks of the enemy.

> Stand therefore, having girded your waist with truth, having put on the breastplate of righteousness, and having shod your feet with the preparation of the gospel of peace; above all, taking the shield of faith with which you will be able to quench all the fiery darts of the wicked one. And take the helmet of salvation, and the **sword of the Spirit**, which is **the word of God**...
>
> Ephesians 6:14-17; emphases mine

In the world of sports, coaches often tell their teams, "Offense wins games; defense wins championships." Such is the value of defense—of protective armor pieces.

Men of war know this. That is partly the reason why Saul wanted David to wear his own armor in the battle against the giant.

David, the man after God's own heart, knew better. This is what he had to say to the giant:

Then David said to the Philistine, "You come to me with a sword, with a spear, and with a javelin. But I come to you in the name of the LORD of hosts, the God of the armies of Israel, whom you have defied. This day the LORD will deliver you into my hand, and I will strike you and take your head from you. And this day I will give the carcasses of the camp of the Philistines to the birds of the air and the wild beasts of the earth, that all the earth may know that there is a God in Israel. Then all this assembly shall know that **the LORD does not save with sword and spear**; for **the battle is the LORD's**, and He will give you into our hands."

I Samuel 17:45-47; emphases mine

This is quite a bold statement coming from a young boy before a giant. But David's confidence did not come from himself or from any human being. His confidence was rooted in his knowledge of God Almighty.

The LORD is my rock and **my fortress** and my deliverer; My God, my strength, in whom I will trust; My shield and the horn of my salvation, my stronghold.

Psalms 18:2; emphasis mine

In another psalm attributed to him, David declared that God is more than an armor. David knew that he did not need an armor made by human hands for God was his fortress!

How about us, modern-day Christians? Can we be confident like David?

Going back to the whole armor of God. The biggest part of the armor (apart from the shield) is the breastplate. It is usually made of thick metal designed to protect the torso. Remember, the torso holds the heart and other vital organs. In a moving human target, the torso is also the widest area to land an attack on. That's why soldiers almost always aim for the torso.

Paul calls this piece of the armor the breastplate of righteousness. Righteousness is the measure of how morally upright a person is—it is what others see in us, in our behavior, in the way we speak and do things. Like the real breastplate, our righteousness is the logical target in the battle. When the enemy sees a "chink in the armor" of our righteousness, he would use it against us.

Is our righteousness strong enough to withstand enemy attacks?

> As it is written: "There is none righteous, no, not one..."
>
> Romans 3:10

If no one is righteous, from whom do we draw our righteousness? How can our breastplate be strong enough?

> He made Christ who knew no sin to [judicially] be sin on our behalf, so that in Him we would become the righteousness of God [that is, we would be made acceptable to Him and placed in a right relationship with Him by His gracious lovingkindness].
>
> 2 Corinthians 5:21 AMP

From Jesus. The strongest breastplate we can have is the righteousness of Jesus reflected in our lives.

In order to keep the breastplate in place, a warrior wears a belt around his waist to fasten the armor to his torso. This part of the armor Paul calls the belt of truth. Our righteousness can only be impenetrable if, and only if, it is held in place by the truth.

> Jesus said to him, "I am the way, **the truth**, and the life. No one comes to the Father except through Me."
>
> John 14:6; emphasis mine

The answer, again, is Jesus. Our righteousness should be rooted in the truth of Jesus Christ.

Next are the boots of peace. We are warriors but we are called to be peacemakers.

> "Blessed are the peacemakers, For they shall be called sons of God."
>
> Matthew 5:9

And who is the Prince of Peace?

> For unto us a Child is born, Unto us a Son is given; And the government will be upon His shoulder. And His name will be called Wonderful, Counselor, Mighty God, Everlasting Father, **Prince of Peace**.
>
> Isaiah 9:6; emphasis mine

As prophesied by the Prophet Isaiah, the Prince of Peace is Jesus. And we are His peacekeeping force in full battle gears.

The next protective gear is the shield of faith. Now the meaning of the word "faith" has been watered down in recent years. There was a time when "faith" almost always refers to faith in God. But not anymore. Faith can now mean faith in oneself; faith in the process or system; faith in other people; faith in the universe.

If I were to make a shield for battle, I want to make it out of the strongest material available. Similarly, faith should be based on something—or Someone—eternal.

> In the beginning was the Word, and the Word was with God, and the Word was God. He was in the beginning with God. All things were made through Him, and without Him nothing was made that was made.
>
> John 1:1-3

These verses, of course, refer to Jesus—the Word who became flesh.

> And the Word became flesh and dwelt among us, and we beheld His glory, the glory as of the only begotten of the Father, full of grace and truth.
>
> John 1:14

Our faith in Jesus is the shield that covers us from the attacks of the enemy.

Now about salvation: no other historical figure can claim to have saved the world. No one but Jesus.

> Nor is there salvation in any other, for there is no other name under heaven given among men by which we must be saved.
>
> Acts 4:12

The helmet of salvation also points to Jesus.

In my college years, one of the computer games that my peers played was CounterStrike. It is a first-person-shooting game where one team acts as the terrorists; the other, the counter-terrorists. In the game, you get to choose the weapons you bring into the skirmishes. Depending on the type of weapon—whether a handgun or an assault rifle—your hit points, which is the measure of how much life you have, will be proportionately reduced when you get hit in certain parts of your body. But when you get hit in the head, regardless of the type of weapon used by the shooter, your hit points are automatically reduced to zero. Then, you are booted out of the game.

In the Great War, we should do everything to keep our helmet of salvation in place. Otherwise, we will lose—the battle and our lives.

And now for the only weapon in the whole armor—the sword. The poet who said, "The pen is mightier than the sword," may have been familiar with Scripture—the penned Word of God.

For the word of God is living and powerful, and sharper than any two-edged sword, piercing even to the division of soul and spirit, and of joints and marrow, and is a discerner of the thoughts and intents of the heart.

Hebrews 4:12

The sword of the Spirit is the Word of God—which is sharper that any two-edged sword. Again, Jesus is the Word who became flesh.

All the pieces of the whole armor fit together like puzzle pieces that form the arsenal with which God provided His warriors. They all point to one name.

For us modern-day Christians, every piece of our armor is none but Jesus.

David derived his strength and protection from God Almighty (Jesus was not yet revealed during his time) whom he likened to a fortress. We shall derive strength and protection from Jesus—the name above all names!

Our humble beginnings are never a hindrance to our higher calling. If we ever find ourselves in a standoff, we just need to reconnect to our cause—our biggest "why"—in order to surmount any giant standing before us. And having Jesus in us is wearing the whole armor of God. He gives us the strength to fight any battle—even against a giant.

THE INTERCEPTOR

NUMBERS 16

An interceptor generally means someone or something that intercepts. But more specifically, it is an aircraft or missile designed to be fast and be able to stop or fend off enemy aircrafts or missiles.

In 2021, during the pandemic, images and videos of missile attacks on Israel intercepted by the "Iron Dome" defense system dominated international news. As reported, 90% of the missile attacks that would have landed on Israeli communities were successfully intercepted by the system. One could only imagine how many human lives could have been lost if not for the interceptors.

Such is the value of interceptors. More so in spiritual warfare.

In Numbers 16, we read about two succeeding events where God's wrath consumed several people. Here, we see how everything that God does—even in His wrath—presents an opportunity for us to know Him more and to grow spiritually.

THE OPERATING PROCEDURE

God is a God of order. In the beginning of time, He set the universe in order. In His dealings, He operates in a set of operating procedures that are beyond human comprehension.

> For God is not a God of disorder but of peace—as in all the congregations of the Lord's people.
>
> 1 Corinthians 14:33 NIV

God's design vs. human traditions

What we humans set in tradition, even in the most conservative Judeo-Christian ones, are only a product of our limited view of God's grand design of things.

In the Jewish culture during Old Testament times, tradition was front and center when it comes to family matters. This was especially true in regard to the firstborn son. The firstborn son takes preeminence over his younger brothers. The firstborn son also gets a double portion of the inheritance from the father.

Remember in *The Warrior*, when Samuel immediately thought that the LORD had chosen Eliab, the firstborn of Jesse? But God had other plans. God chose the eighth son, David, to be the next king. This seems contradictory to the tradition of the people. However, tradition was also seemingly upended in the case of the sons of Jacob as evidenced by how he bequeathed blessings to them.

Jacob had twelve sons. The firstborn was Reuben—his son with his first wife, Leah. In the end, Reuben did not get the preeminence and the double portion which were traditionally reserved for the firstborn.

Preeminence went to Judah.

In his dying bed in Egypt, Jacob blessed his twelve sons. We read *this* towards the end of the book of Genesis.

"**Judah, you are he whom your brothers shall praise**; Your hand shall be on the neck of your enemies; **Your father's children shall bow down before you.** Judah is a lion's whelp; From the prey, my son, you have gone up. He bows down, he lies down as a lion;

And as a lion, who shall rouse him? **The scepter shall not depart from Judah**, Nor a lawgiver from between his feet, Until Shiloh comes; And to Him shall be the obedience of the people. Binding his donkey to the vine, And his donkey's colt to the choice vine, He washed his garments in wine, And his clothes in the blood of grapes. His eyes are darker than wine, And his teeth whiter than milk."

Genesis 49:8-12; emphases mine

The tribe of Judah would later become the bloodline of kings. From his lineage would come King David—the man after God's own heart. Jacob's blessings came true through David whose kingdom God established forever.

And your house and your kingdom shall be established forever before you. Your throne shall be established forever.

II Samuel 7:16

Recall that one of the main premises of this book is that God relegated dominion over His creation to man. By doing so, He also gave man free will.

Solomon succeeded his father to the throne. He started out well and became the wisest king when he asked God for wisdom over riches, honor, and long life. But abuse of free will led Solomon to his eventual demise. He was turned away from God by his many wives. Solomon's fall eventually led to the division of the kingdom.

> For it was so, when Solomon was old, that his wives turned his heart after other gods; and his heart was not loyal to the LORD his God, as was the heart of his father David.
>
> Therefore the LORD said to Solomon, "Because you have done this, and have not kept My covenant and My statutes, which I have commanded you, I will surely tear the kingdom away from you and give it to your servant. Nevertheless I will not do it in your days, for the sake of your father David; I will tear it out of the hand of your son. However I will not tear away the whole kingdom; I will give one tribe to your son for the sake of My servant David, and for the sake of Jerusalem which I have chosen."
>
> I Kings 11:4, 11-13

Again, God always stays true to His word. He kept His promise to David. His word is always true.

So from the time of Solomon, the kingdom was divided into two: Israel, the Northern Kingdom, and Judah, the Southern Kingdom. David's descendants

—all from the bloodline of Judah—would rule over the Southern Kingdom until the people were exiled to Babylon.

Again, Judah received the blessing of preeminence.

According to the laws of Moses, the firstborn son was to get a double portion of inheritance also.

> If a man has two wives, one loved and the other unloved, and they have borne him children, both the loved and the unloved, and if the firstborn son is of her who is unloved, then it shall be, on the day he bequeaths his possessions to his sons, that he must not bestow firstborn status on the son of the loved wife in preference to the son of the unloved, the true firstborn. But he shall acknowledge the son of the unloved wife as the firstborn by giving him a double portion of all that he has, for he is the beginning of his strength; the right of the firstborn is his.
>
> Deuteronomy 21:15-17

In the case of Jacob's sons, the double portion of blessings went to Joseph. Before Jacob blessed his own sons, he adopted Joseph's sons, Ephraim and Manasseh, to be his own.

And now your two sons, Ephraim and Manasseh, who were born to you in the land of Egypt before I came to you in Egypt, are mine; as Reuben and Simeon, they shall be mine.

Genesis 48:5

Ephraim and Manasseh each received blessings from Jacob. Thus, technically, two portions of blessings went to Joseph.

And he blessed Joseph, and said: "God, before whom my fathers Abraham and Isaac walked, The God who has fed me all my life long to this day, The Angel who has redeemed me from all evil, **Bless the lads**; Let my name be named upon them, And the name of my fathers Abraham and Isaac; And let them grow into a multitude in the midst of the earth."

Genesis 48:15-16; emphasis mine

Moses' successor as leader was Joshua, an Ephraimite. The tribe of Ephraim continued to rise in prominence during the time of the Judges as it became the head of the ten northern tribes (even before the kingdom was divided). Then, as Deborah, the prophetess, judged Israel, "she would sit under the palm tree of Deborah between Ramah and Bethel in the mountains of Ephraim. And the children of Israel came up to her for judgment" (Judges 4:5).

The Ark of the Covenant also stayed for a long time at Shiloh which was in the territory of Ephraim.

By the time of the prophet Isaiah, the tribe of Ephraim had become synonymous to the ten northern tribes.

> Ephraim and Judah will [unite and] swoop down on the slopes of the Philistines toward the west; Together they will plunder the sons (Arabs) of the east. They will possess Edom and Moab, And the sons of Ammon will be subject to them.
>
> Isaiah 11:14 AMP

The Tribe of Manasseh on the other hand grew in number. So much so that they were the only tribe to settle on both the east and west sides of the Jordan. Their geographic territory was the widest among all tribes.

The half-tribe of Manasseh was given territories on the east side of the Jordan before they entered the Promised Land. On their way into Canaan, the Israelites had to conquer the kings and lands east of the Jordan. The sons of Reuben and the sons of

Gad wanted to settle there because they had so many livestock. It would appear that the same was the case for Manasseh.

> Now the children of Reuben and the children of Gad had a very great multitude of livestock; and when they saw the land of Jazer and the land of Gilead, that indeed the region was a place for livestock, the children of Gad and the children of Reuben came and spoke to Moses, to Eleazar the priest, and to the leaders of the congregation, saying, "Ataroth, Dibon, Jazer, Nimrah, Heshbon, Elealeh, Shebam, Nebo, and Beon, the country which the LORD defeated before the congregation of Israel, is a land for livestock, and your servants have livestock." Therefore they said, "If we have found favor in your sight, let this land be given to your servants as a possession. Do not take us over the Jordan."
>
> So Moses gave to the children of Gad, to the children of Reuben, and to **half the tribe of Manasseh** the son of Joseph, the kingdom of Sihon king of the Amorites and the kingdom of Og king of Bashan, the land with its cities within the borders, the cities of the surrounding country.

Numbers 32:1-5, 33; emphasis mine

Again, the preeminence and double portion reserved for the firstborn son didn't go to Reuben. It may have something to do with how Reuben conducted himself—having slept with Bilhah, the concubine of his father.

> And it happened, when Israel dwelt in that land, that Reuben went and lay with Bilhah his father's concubine; and Israel heard about it. Now the sons of Jacob were twelve...
>
> Genesis 35:22

Jacob did not forget the act as reflected in his last words for Reuben.

> "Reuben, you are my firstborn; My might, the beginning of my strength and vigor, Preeminent in dignity and preeminent in power [that should have been your birthright]. But unstable and reckless and boiling over like water [in sinful lust], you shall not excel or have the preeminence [of the firstborn], Because you went up to your father's bed [with Bilhah]; You defiled it—he went up to my couch."
>
> Genesis 49:3-4 AMP

However, as the family tree of Jacob would prove, God operates above human traditions. God chose Isaac over Ishmael; Jacob over Esau; Judah and Joseph over Reuben; Ephraim over Manasseh (who was Joseph's firstborn); Moses over Aaron; David over all his brothers. It doesn't mean God does not honor human traditions—He is just above any and all of them.

The Apostle Paul actually uses the analogy of the firstborn to exalt Jesus.

> He is the image of the invisible God, **the firstborn of all creation**; for in him all things in heaven and on earth were created, things visible and invisible, whether thrones or dominions or rulers or powers—all things have been created through him and for him. He himself is before all things, and in him all things hold together.

> Colossians 1:15-17 NRSV; emphasis mine

God's promise to David that his "throne will be established forever," was fully fulfilled in Jesus. That is why those who were waiting for the coming of the Messiah referred to Him as the "Son of David." In addition, Jacob's blessing for Judah that "the scepter shall not depart from [him]" is also fully fulfilled in Jesus—the King of kings.

Both David and Jesus were from the line of Judah.

> He will be great, and will be called the Son of
> the Highest; and the Lord God will give Him
> the throne of His father David. And He will
> reign over the house of Jacob forever, and of
> His kingdom there will be no end.

> Luke 1:32-33

The LORD does not dislike human traditions, per se.
He dislikes the human tendency to hold traditions
higher than they ought to be held.

> Then the Lord said, "Because this nation
> approaches [Me only] with their words And
> honors Me [only] with their lip service, But
> they remove their hearts far from Me, And
> their reverence for Me is a tradition that is
> learned by rote [without any regard for its
> meaning], Therefore, listen carefully, I will
> again do marvelous and amazing things with
> this people, wonderful and astonishing
> things; And the wisdom of their wise men will
> perish, And the understanding of their
> discerning men will be hidden."

> Isaiah 29:13-14 AMP

God had shown that indeed He is above all.

In Numbers 16, Korah and his company, in a sense, questioned God's design of the priesthood. God had already set aside the Levites to serve in the Tabernacle. Korah, a Levite, also sought after the priesthood which was reserved for a particular clan in the tribe of the Levites—the bloodline of Aaron. Korah's argument was that since they were all people of God, then they were all on equal footing.

> They gathered together against Moses and Aaron, and said to them, "You take too much upon yourselves, for all the congregation is holy, every one of them, and the LORD is among them. Why then do you exalt yourselves above the assembly of the LORD?"
>
> Numbers 16:3

This is a direct affront against God's design. But Moses, surely with the empowering of God, saw right through Korah and his company.

> Then Moses said to Korah, "Hear now, you sons of Levi: Is it a small thing to you that the God of Israel has separated you from the congregation of Israel, to bring you near to Himself, to do the work of the tabernacle of

the LORD, and to stand before the congregation to serve them; and that He has brought you near to Himself, you and all your brethren, the sons of Levi, with you? And are you seeking the priesthood also? Therefore you and all your company are gathered together against the LORD. And what is Aaron that you complain against him?"

Numbers 16:8-11

This is huge because it was the same desire to rise higher than what God designed that caused the fall of Lucifer.

"How you are fallen from heaven, O Lucifer, son of the morning! How you are cut down to the ground, You who weakened the nations! For you have said in your heart: 'I will ascend into heaven, I will exalt my throne above the stars of God; I will also sit on the mount of the congregation On the farthest sides of the north; I will ascend above the heights of the clouds, I will be like the Most High.'"

Isaiah 14:12-14

Why did God command the building of the Tabernacle? What was God's intention? What was His intended design?

"And let them make Me a sanctuary, that I may dwell among them."

Exodus 25:8

God wanted to have a sanctuary where He could dwell among His people. That sanctuary was a physical place in Old Testament times. The priesthood was established because the sinfulness of the people could not handle the holiness of God. The priests became the intermediaries.

The priesthood, however, later became corrupted by tradition. But it (the priesthood) was God's design at that point in history.

When Jesus was revealed, He basically upended this structure. Remember, He is the High Priest in the order of Melchizedek. He simply reverted back to the intended design what human traditions had corrupted.

The Tabernacle was a place where God may dwell with the people. Jesus is Immanuel—God with us. Jesus made the Tabernacle (which later became the Temple) more accessible to all. He came to become the sanctuary where God would meet His people. It's no longer a geographical location; it's now a Person.

"Behold, the virgin shall be with child, and bear a Son, and they shall call His name Immanuel," which is translated, "God with us."

Matthew 1:23

Jesus became our access to God.

Again, God's design over and above human traditions.

God's timing vs. human convenience

When Moses called on Dathan and Abiram, the companions of Korah, they did not come up. Instead, they uttered their own complaints.

And Moses sent to call Dathan and Abiram the sons of Eliab, but they said, "We will not come up! Is it a small thing that you have brought us up out of a land flowing with milk and honey, to kill us in the wilderness, that **you should keep acting like a prince over us**? Moreover **you have not brought us into a land flowing with milk and honey, nor given us inheritance of fields and vineyards**. Will you put out the eyes of these men? We will not come up!"

Numbers 16:12-14; emphases mine

It would seem that these two also had that same insolent attitude—they refused to honor the structure that God had ordained, and they refused to follow the leader that God had chosen. But they added more to their complaint. Aside from questioning the positions of Moses and Aaron, they also laid bare their impatience. They couldn't wait to get hold of their inheritance.

In essence, the people complained about God's timing by gauging it against their convenience.

At this point, the people had spent more than a year in the wilderness. And they had just made a big mistake when they refused to conquer the Promised Land because of the unfavorable reports of ten of the twelve spies (read Numbers 13 and 14). And for that, they were now facing 40 years of wandering in the wilderness. With the problems they had met so far, they may have feared that there would be more inconveniences ahead.

The people did not understand that God was building them up as a nation. Their nationhood may have been forged in slavery in Egypt, but it was in the wilderness that God was "fortifying" them as a nation. God was preparing them for their conquest. Their advance in the wilderness was slow because their conquest would also be little by little.

"I will not drive them out from before you in one year, lest the land become desolate and the beasts of the field become too numerous for you. Little by little I will drive them out from before you, until you have increased, and you inherit the land."

Exodus 23:29-30

It may be said that civilization has advanced because of humanity's endless quest for convenience. And that is totally fine. In fact, knowledge and wisdom come from God.

For the LORD gives wisdom; From His mouth come knowledge and understanding;

Proverbs 2:6

Using our God-given wisdom, knowledge, and skills for the good of all is never wrong.

In the narrative, the people tried to circumvent what God had already declared. They were to spend 40 years in the wilderness as a result of their disobedience. In addition, the grown ups who have witnessed God's wonders in Egypt were forbidden to enter the Promised Land.

"The carcasses of you who have complained against Me shall fall in this wilderness, all of you who were numbered, according to your entire number, from twenty years old and above. Except for Caleb the son of Jephunneh and Joshua the son of Nun, you shall by no means enter the land which I swore I would make you dwell in. But your little ones, whom you said would be victims, I will bring in, and they shall know the land which you have despised. But as for you, your carcasses shall fall in this wilderness. And your sons shall be shepherds in the wilderness forty years, and bear the brunt of your infidelity, until your carcasses are consumed in the wilderness. According to the number of the days in which you spied out the land, forty days, for each day you shall bear your guilt one year, namely forty years, and you shall know My rejection. I the LORD have spoken this. I will surely do so to all this evil congregation who are gathered together against Me. In this wilderness they shall be consumed, and there they shall die."

Numbers 14:29-35

And yet, they demanded to get their inheritance right there and then. If that is not being impatient with God's timing, I don't know what is.

God's sovereignty vs. human wisdom

After the Korah incident, one would think that the people had somehow learned that God is above everything. Korah and his company sure did learn the hard way, but it was too late for them.

> Now it came to pass, as he finished speaking all these words, that the ground split apart under them, and the earth opened its mouth and swallowed them up, with their households and all the men with Korah, with all their goods. So they and all those with them went down alive into the pit; the earth closed over them, and they perished from among the assembly.
>
> And a fire came out from the LORD and consumed the two hundred and fifty men who were offering incense.
>
> Numbers 16:31-33, 35

However, the people came up to Moses and Aaron accusing them of murder. It's as though they had completely forgotten what they witnessed before their eyes the day before.

> On the next day all the congregation of the children of Israel complained against Moses and Aaron, saying, "You have killed the people of the LORD."
>
> Numbers 16:41

It's as if they denied that it was God Himself who made the decision to put an end to Korah and his company—it was God who caused the ground to open to swallow up Korah and his household; it was God who sent fire to consume the 250 men who were offering incense.

Time and again, the people's wisdom seemed unable to grasp around the sovereignty of God.

In *The Warrior*, we made reference to a verse in Ecclesiastes 3 where we put emphasis on the first half of the second sentence of the verse. The second half of it pictures the limitation of human comprehension of the works of God. (The first sentence in the passage further supports the previous section on God's timing.)

> He has made everything beautiful in its time. Also He has put eternity in their hearts, except that **no one can find out the work that God does from beginning to end**.
>
> Ecclesiastes 3:11; emphasis mine

Sovereignty is synonymous to ascendancy, dominion, power, and supremacy. Even the sum of all those synonyms could never fully define God's sovereignty.

Job put it eloquently:

If one wished to contend with Him,

He could not answer Him one time out of a thousand.

God is wise in heart and mighty in strength.

Who has hardened himself against Him and prospered?

He removes the mountains, and they do not know

When He overturns them in His anger;

He shakes the earth out of its place,

And its pillars tremble;

He commands the sun, and it does not rise;

He seals off the stars;

He alone spreads out the heavens,

And treads on the waves of the sea;

He made the Bear, Orion, and the Pleiades,

And the chambers of the south;

He does great things past finding out,

Yes, wonders without number.

If He goes by me, I do not see Him;

If He moves past, I do not perceive Him;

If He takes away, who can hinder Him?

Who can say to Him, 'What are You doing?'

Job 9:3-12

An affront to God's design and timing is an affront to God's sovereignty.

THE DIVIDE

The role of the interceptor is to stand in the gap—in the divide. In any organization, there could be countless divides based on beliefs, ideologies, methodologies, preferences, and many other conflicting ideas. The most critical of all is where we are called to: the divide between life and death.

We have already established early on that we are in the midst of the Great War. Good, truth, light, and life are on one side; evil, falsehood, darkness, and death, on the other. This is the great divide. All wars on different levels of life and society boil down to this war. And there are only two sides.

> "You are a king, then!" said Pilate. Jesus answered, "You say that I am a king. In fact, the reason I was born and came into the world is to testify to the truth. Everyone **on the side of truth** listens to me."
>
> John 18:37 NIV; emphasis mine

The verse above is part of the conversation Jesus had with Pilate. In the account of John, Jesus explicitly declared that the reason He was born was to testify to the truth and that those on the side of truth listens to Him. If truth is on one side, what's on the other side?

> Jesus said to them, "If God were your Father, you would love Me, for I proceeded forth and came from God; nor have I come of Myself, but He sent Me. Why do you not understand My speech? Because you are not able to listen to My word. **You are of your father the devil**, and the desires of your father you want to do. **He was a murderer from the beginning, and does not stand in the truth, because there is no truth in him**. When he speaks a lie, he speaks from his own resources, for he is a liar and the father of it."
>
> John 8:42-44; emphases mine

In the preceding verse, Jesus tells of the other side of the divide. For context, Jesus was talking to Pharisees who had categorically refused to believe in Him. He deliberately told them that their father was the devil.

Again, the Great War only has two sides. Choosing the right side is an imperative.

When the Philistines, with their champion Goliath of Gath, went up against Israel, the battle scene was literally the picture of the great divide.

The Philistines stood on a mountain on one
side, and Israel stood on a mountain on the
other side, with a valley between them.

I Samuel 17:3

The world's wisdom of today tells us to choose our
battle—choose battles where there is a bigger
possibility of winning. But that's not what David did.
In fact, he chose to fight a battle that no one would
dare choose—to fight the giant in one-on-one
combat. I firmly believe that it was easy for him to
do so because instead of choosing his battles, he
chose a side—the side of light, truth, life, and good;
the side where God is glorified!

And so, Aaron stood in the gap between the living
and the dead—between life and death. He did not
do it so he could avoid choosing a side. He did it to
protect the living from dying. He intercepted the
spread of the plague to save the people from
death.

David stepped into the divide to prevent the
advance of the enemy. Aaron stepped into the
divide to stop the spread of the plague. The giant
and the plague were but agents of death. And there
was one Man who stepped into the divide to
conquer death once and for all: Jesus.

But now [as things really are] Christ has in fact been raised from the dead, [and He became] the first fruits [that is, the first to be resurrected with an incorruptible, immortal body, foreshadowing the resurrection] of those who have fallen asleep [in death]. For since [it was] by a man that death came [into the world], it is also by a Man that the resurrection of the dead has come. For just as in Adam all die, so also in Christ all will be made alive.

The last enemy to be abolished and put to an end is death.

1 Corinthians 15:20-22, 26 AMP

Jesus has already won for us the victory. Until Jesus comes again, the enemy will always try to keep us away from that truth. And that is why the world still needs interceptors.

Are we bold enough to stand in the divide?

THE PREPARATORY REQUISITES

What does it take to stand in the gap?

So Moses said to Aaron, "Take a censer and put fire in it from the altar, put incense on it, and take it quickly to the congregation and make atonement for them; for wrath has gone out from the LORD. The plague has begun." Then Aaron took it as Moses commanded, and ran into the midst of the assembly; and already the plague had begun among the people. So he put in the incense and made atonement for the people. And he stood between the dead and the living; so the plague was stopped.

Numbers 16:46-48

Anyone who wants to be used by God for His purpose can stand in the gap as long as he is fully prepared for whatever the task entails.

Be spiritually prepared

Among the Levites, Aaron's bloodline was given the priesthood. But that does not mean they can disregard the rigorous requirements of administering their priestly duties. Two of the earliest priests—the two sons of Aaron—failed to suffice the requirements.

Then Nadab and Abihu, the sons of Aaron, each took his censer and put fire in it, put incense on it, and offered profane fire before the LORD, which He had not commanded them. So fire went out from the LORD and devoured them, and they died before the LORD.

Leviticus 10:1-2

It is not clear what made the fire profane. Nadab and Abihu may have used incense that was not according to God's specification.

> And the LORD said to Moses: "Take sweet spices, stacte and onycha and galbanum, and pure frankincense with these sweet spices; there shall be equal amounts of each. You shall make of these an incense, a compound according to the art of the perfumer, salted, pure, and holy. And you shall beat some of it very fine, and put some of it before the Testimony in the tabernacle of meeting where I will meet with you. It shall be most holy to you.
>
> Exodus 30:34-36

These preparations may be physical in nature, but I believe they were a foreshadowing of what Jesus said in the Sermon on the Mount.

> "Therefore if you bring your gift to the altar, and there remember that your brother has something against you, leave your gift there before the altar, and go your way. First be reconciled to your brother, and then come and offer your gift."
>
> Matthew 5:23-24

There is no room for profanity in God's altar. In the Old Testament, it was about the right specification of everything offered in the altar; in the New Testament, it's about having the right heart.

What happened to Nadab and Abihu shows that God's specifications are not to be taken lightly. But God is also a God of grace. Throughout history, He has reached out to His people to help them understand His heart.

> "I will give you a new heart and put a new spirit within you; I will take the heart of stone out of your flesh and give you a heart of flesh. I will put My Spirit within you and cause you to walk in My statutes, and you will keep My judgments and do them."
>
> Ezekiel 36:26-27

Anyone with the right spirit can stand in the gap.

Be physically prepared

In Numbers 16, Aaron ran to take fire from the altar and to stand in the midst of the assembly. Run— that is impressive for a man who's more than 80 years old. Not all old men could do that; not all young men could do that.

We have to be physically prepared also.

Jesus warned his disciples about this in the Garden of Gethsemane when He found them sleeping while He was praying. This was before He was arrested.

> "Watch and pray, lest you enter into temptation. The spirit indeed is willing, but the flesh is weak."

> Matthew 26:41

When our son turned two, my wife and I enrolled him to a gym class for kids. For his age group, classes were parent-child sessions. So, I had to go in with him. The first question that came to mind was, "Will I be able to keep up with his energy?" The next question was, "When he starts to play sports, will I be able to play with him or do training drills with him?"

So I finally decided to do regular exercises so that I can be there for him whenever he needs me. I knew that moral support would not be enough. He would need someone who will play, train, and practice with him. And I decided that that someone should be me. My spirit had always been willing to run with him, but I knew that my flesh was weak, hence, I needed to be physically prepared.

Now, I make sure I run and do workouts for at least an hour everyday (under normal circumstances).

Aaron was born into slavery. Before God's delivery through Moses, he might have been doing hard labor all day. I think it's safe to say that he was physically strong.

Without knowing it, he was training his body for a more important role. Even if all those physical labor built his body just so he could run to the midst of the assembly to stop the plague, it would have been worth it. It's one thing to be an instrument of God's might. It's entirely another to be an instrument of His grace.

We have to be prepared spiritually and physically.

Be logistically prepared

Logistics is defined as the detailed coordination, and subsequent harmonization, of several people, facilities, or supplies to perform a complex operation.

This is what the Apostle Paul wrote about in his letter to the Corinthians about 2,000 years ago about the Church—the body of Christ.

> But now indeed there are many members, yet one body. And the eye cannot say to the hand, "I have no need of you"; nor again the head to the feet, "I have no need of you." No, much rather, those members of the body which seem to be weaker are necessary. And

those members of the body which we think to be less honorable, on these we bestow greater honor; and our unpresentable parts have greater modesty, but our presentable parts have no need. But God composed the body, having given greater honor to that part which lacks it, that there should be no schism in the body, but that the members should have the same care for one another. And if one member suffers, all the members suffer with it; or if one member is honored, all the members rejoice with it. Now you are the body of Christ, and members individually.

I Corinthians 12:20-27

Aaron, as well as Moses, understood this centuries earlier—way before the Church of Christ was established. They understood that they were part of the logistics in serving God and that if a part of the logistics suffers, all parts suffer with it. If not, Aaron wouldn't have taken orders from his younger brother, Moses, whom God had chosen to lead the people; he wouldn't have intercepted the plague to keep it from spreading further to more people.

But the organization of the body of Christ is not meant to be bureaucratic. It's meant to be a community.

Therefore if there is any consolation in Christ, if any comfort of love, if any fellowship of the Spirit, if any affection and mercy, fulfill my joy by being like-minded, having the same love, being of one accord, of one mind. Let nothing be done through selfish ambition or conceit, but in lowliness of mind let each esteem others better than himself. Let each of you look out not only for his own interests, but also for the interests of others.

Philippians 2:1-4

In the Korah incident, Moses told the Levite and his company to present themselves before the LORD. When Dathan and Abiram refused, he got angry.

Then Moses was very angry, and said to the LORD, "Do not respect their offering. I have not taken one donkey from them, nor have I hurt one of them."

Numbers 16:15

When God was about to consume the entire congregation with fire, Moses intervened.

And the LORD spoke to Moses and Aaron, saying, "Separate yourselves from among this congregation, that I may consume them in a moment." Then they fell on their faces, and said, "O God, the God of the spirits of all flesh, shall one man sin, and You be angry with all the congregation?"

Numbers 16:20-22

I believe that God's intention was not to display His power and the consequences of His wrath. Rather, He wanted His chosen ones to emulate His steadfast love for His people.

So on the next day, when the congregation came again to complain, God's wrath was roused once more. This time, Moses did not give in to his anger anymore like he did a number of times before. He and Aaron had learned how to emulate the love of God. That was when Moses directed Aaron to be the interceptor.

This seamlessly connects to what Jesus said in New Testament times. When He was about to go up to Jerusalem He told His disciples more about what it is like in His kingdom.

But Jesus called them to Himself and said, "You know that the rulers of the Gentiles lord it over them, and those who are great exercise authority over them. Yet it shall not be so among you; but whoever desires to become great among you, let him be your servant. And whoever desires to be first among you, let him be your slave— just as the Son of Man did not come to be served, but to serve, and to give His life a ransom for many."

Matthew 20:25-28

If ever you feel unprepared for service, logistically or otherwise, just remember what Jesus did on earth and what He told His disciples.

"By this all will know that you are My disciples, if you have love for one another."

John 13:35

God's standard operating procedure is above human comprehension. After all, He is sovereign. All we need to do is understand His love and emulate it. When we do, we can be prepared to stand in the divide in His name and for His purpose.

THE CONQUERORS

DEUTERONOMY 11:10-15

A conqueror is one who surmounts challenges and opposition to win a cause. In a cruder definition, a conqueror is one who uses military force to gain control over a land or a people.

On May 29, 1953, the summit of Mount Everest, the world's tallest mountain, was conquered by Sir Edmund Hillary. Before then, several attempts had been made since 1921 by at least ten team expeditions.

Hillary would be remembered in history as the first man to step onto the summit of the highest mountain in the world. But he was not alone in his conquest. Aside from his Sherpa[6] counterpart, Tenzing Norgay, who was with him at the summit, he was part of a team led by Sir John Hunt. The team was composed of "350 porters, 20 Sherpas, and tons of supplies to support a vanguard of only ten climbers.[7]"

Hillary and Norgay were not the only ones from the team who attempted to reach for the summit. In fact, they were the second to make the attempt. The first was only 101 meters short of reaching the top. It was a team effort.

Conquering Mount Everest required a team, just as fighting a war requires an army. This does not only apply to actual wars and conquests. More so, it applies to the Great War.

After the Israelites entered the Promised Land, years of conquest followed. God had given them the land but it was already inhabited. They had to drive out and destroy the inhabitants before they could settle down and claim their inheritance. (Why would God commission such a thing? This will be discussed in *The General* and *The Special Operative*.)

---

[6] The Sherpa are a group of people living in the most mountainous region of Tibet

[7] https://www.nationalgeographic.com/adventure/article/sir-edmund-hillary-tenzing-norgay-1953

THE NEW GROUND

The Israelites were about to end their sojourn around the wilderness and were about to enter the Promised Land. It could be that they did not yet fully understand the situation they were in for. Some of them were born as slaves in Egypt. Most of the older ones had died before reaching Canaan because God did not allow them, including Moses, to enter the land. It could be that a vast majority of the people were born in the wilderness and only experienced life *there*.

> For the land which you go to possess is not like the land of Egypt from which you have come, where you sowed your seed and watered it by foot, as a vegetable garden; but the land which you cross over to possess is a land of hills and valleys, which drinks water from the rain of heaven, a land for which the LORD your God cares; the eyes of the LORD your God are always on it, from the beginning of the year to the very end of the year. 'And it shall be that if you earnestly obey My commandments which I command you today, to love the LORD your God and serve Him with all your heart and with all your soul, then I will give you the rain for your land in its season, the early rain and the latter rain, that you may gather in your grain, your new wine, and your oil. And I will send

grass in your fields for your livestock, that you may eat and be filled.'

Deuteronomy 11:10-15

Everything in the Promised Land was new to the people. And the human brain perceives that anything new always comes with uncertainties.

The topography

God, through Moses, informed the people that the terrain of the land they were entering into was very different from what they had seen or experienced in Egypt. In Egypt, the Israelites occupied the Goshen delta of the Nile. A delta is a land formation at the mouth of a river composed of sediments deposited by the river over several years. As such, deltas are flat. And since the Nile is the longest river on earth, the Goshen delta was vast.

This was in stark contrast to the terrain of the Promised Land, which, as said in the passage above, was composed of hills and valleys.

The land presented a variety of challenges for the people. First, they had to conquer the land by military force. Their ancestor Abraham, at least once, engaged in militia warfare in the Promised Land before their migration to Egypt during the time of Joseph. However, for these people, their experience in doing war was in the wilderness where the terrain was most likely predominantly flat. Fighting on hilly terrain in an uncharted territory could be a major challenge. Cities in the land were likely built on top of hills. They would have to do uphill battles. Anyone who rides a bicycle knows the difficulty of riding uphill.

Second, the people had been provided with manna and quail in the desert for sustenance. As they entered the Promised Land, this divine provision was about to cease, necessitating their need to learn how to procure food on their own. While they would later acquire farms, gardens, and vineyards from the people they would conquer, they would still need to farm *these* themselves. They would also bring in their flocks and herds—which had grown in number since they left Egypt. Farming and grazing in the land could also be difficult for them.

The topography of the land also played a big role in its hydrology.

The hydrology

The Goshen delta in Egypt was a fertile land. The Nile would deposit fertile sediments from the upstream of the river's basin. Thus, farms in the delta were fed with water and fertile soil from the Nile. Having lived in Egypt for centuries, they most certainly have adopted the farming techniques and technology of Egypt—one of the most advanced civilizations at the time. But all would be useless in the new land.

The land they were going to conquer was very dependent on rain. The hilly terrain of the area would mean that the valleys would have small intermittent streams—called "wadi" in the Old Testament. They would have to learn how to utilize rainwater that falls into the land wisely.

I live in a city in the Philippines where urban flooding is a perennial issue. My line of work has taken me to different towns in the country where I have observed similar problems. With my experience, I've become so familiar with the type of rainfall events that cause flooding in urban areas.

Especially in the Cebu metropolitan area, high-intensity rainfall events with short durations are almost always the cause of urban flooding. This is because catchments[8] in the metropolis are small— like those described in Deuteronomy 11. To add to the problem, the natural intermittent streams in the city had long been constrained, obstructed, or otherwise covered by sporadic development.

---

[8] A catchment is an area defined by the configuration of the terrain within which all rainwater drains towards a common point of discharge; a valley is a picture of a catchment: the surrounding mountain ridges define the boundary, rainwater eventually gathers into the river, and the mouth of the river is the discharge point.

Furthermore, most of the catchments or valleys of the intermittent waterways have already been covered with paving or roofing materials. Thus, flooding in urban areas happens almost immediately after an intense rainfall, even with a short duration.

The situation is quite different in places with large river systems—like the Nile River Basin. These rivers have large catchment areas that extend to the mountains. These catchments are often covered with lush vegetation that help delay the onslaught of floods.

One such river system is Mandulog River in Iligan City in the southern island group of Mindanao in the Philippines. I was part of the technical team that made a study for flood control projects on the banks of the river. The study was done a few years after tropical storm Washi (known in the Philippines as Typhoon Sendong) wrecked havoc in December 2011. The devastating flood left 1,600 people dead or missing.

People were literally caught off guard as floodwaters overflowed from the banks of the river. The level of the water was so high it reached the underside of the bridge; the current, laden with mud and debris, was so strong that the bridge broke.

Later, it was reported that on the night the flood reached the city, some people were out and about to celebrate—Christmas 2011 was just around the corner. The weather may have become favorable because it had been raining some days prior.

The weather bureau reported that the flood was brought about by a month's worth of rain that fell over the span of 24 hours. It would seem that the rain continued to fall in the mountains as the people in the city were having their Christmas parties.

While ours in the Philippines are a result of poor planning practices and poor stormwater management, I couldn't help but think that if the Israelites did not bother learning the hydrology of the Promised Land, they could have suffered the same fate. The people had to learn how to properly manage rainwater.

The liberty

But what was really new to the people going into the land was their liberty. A few of them were born in Egypt as slaves. But the vast majority of them (who were entering the land) were born in the wilderness where they were under the leadership of Moses. All of them have not experienced to be a people governing themselves. This may have been the biggest "new" that they would *have* entering the land.

After the years of conquest, the people settled down by tribe into their territories. In the following generations (after Joshua), there would be no central government over the tribes of Israel—until the time of the kings.

Topography, hydrology, and liberty are all gifts from God. Surrounding circumstances may not be the same for all of us, but we are all recipients of these blessings. What we do with them matters more. This burden is especially heavy for those who experience them for the first time in their lives.

There will come a point in our lives when we find ourselves in a new environment where the rules are not the same as the ones that molded us into the person we are at the moment, and where our newfound freedom can be overbearing. In that moment, the very first thing we have to conquer is ourselves. We have to conquer our tendency to conform to what is around us—our tendency to get lost in the new things and forget the purpose for which we have been placed where we are.

Coming from a small town in the province, I experienced this newfound freedom in college—not once, but twice. I spent my college days in Dumaguete City where I lived away from my parents.

I lived even farther away from my family when I spent an entire school year in a university in the suburbs of Tokyo, Japan as a foreign exchange student.

I rarely did anything outside of what was expected of me as a student—like being absent from school or going out with friends at night—simply because I didn't want to disappoint my parents. I strived to excel in class to honor their hard work and sacrifices just so they could send me to a good school. Furthermore, I didn't want to go against the values with which my brother and I were raised.

It's only after I became an adult when I realized that not many people have handled their newfound liberty well. I do not claim that I did not stray from the path set by the core values inculcated to me, but I would say that staying the course took a lot of courage and discipline. To not give in to peer pressure, or to all other external forces, was a feat in itself.

The Israelites were tasked to conquer the former inhabitants of the land. It took them years to get a good grip of their territory. But even so, they left some areas unconquered. Topography and hydrology—physical constraints—may have been good alibis for their failure. But more often than not, it was their shortcoming in a deeper, more personal level, that dragged them down—their failure to handle of the liberty entrusted to them.

> In those days there was no king in Israel; everyone did what was right in his own eyes.
>
> Judges 17:6

Many times they used their newfound freedom to sin against God. By the time of the judges, people did whatever they saw fit.

THE SUPPLY

Like many times in the past, the people forgot what God had commanded: to obey His commandments and to love and serve Him with all their heart and with all their soul (Deuteronomy 11:13). Forgetting this command means forfeiting the promise that comes with it—that He would give them the early and the latter rain so that they would have grain, new wine, and oil (Deuteronomy 11:14).

It was their forefather—Abraham, the father of faith —who first acknowledged God as Jehovah-Jireh, the LORD will provide. It was during the time when Isaac, his son, asked him about the sacrifice they were to offer to God on the mountain. They had prepared everything except the sacrificial animal. With bold faith, Abraham declared that God will provide! And it was indeed so.

But Isaac spoke to Abraham his father and said, "My father!" And he said, "Here I am, my son." Then he said, "Look, the fire and the wood, but where is the lamb for a burnt offering?" And Abraham said, "My son, God will provide for Himself the lamb for a burnt offering." So the two of them went together.

And He said, "Do not lay your hand on the lad, or do anything to him; for now I know that you fear God, since you have not withheld your son, your only son, from Me." Then Abraham lifted his eyes and looked, and there behind him was a ram caught in a thicket by its horns. So Abraham went and took the ram, and offered it up for a burnt offering instead of his son.

Genesis 22:7-8, 12-13

God's promise was not one of sustenance only but also of abundance. He promised to supply the rain needed for them to gather in grain, new wine, and oil. Each of these had different significance in the life of the people.

But the key that unlocks this promise is obedience. God provided Abraham with the ram for the burnt offering only after he obeyed and brought his son to be sacrificed. It's the same for the conquering Israelites. It's the same for us.

Grain

The main ingredient of bread, their staple food, was grain. In essence, God promised physical sustenance to the conquerors. As soon as they entered the land, manna stopped falling from the sky. In its place, God promised rain to fall so that their fields would grow grain.

Many of us fear to venture into something new—to put up a new business, to move to a new city, to own up to new responsibilities, or to do anything we are not accustomed to—because we might not be able to sustain it. Or worse, we might not be able to sustain ourselves and our family.

Too often we find ourselves settling for what we currently have, even though it is barely enough or not interesting enough for us anymore. This is because we fear that if we step out of our comfort zone, we might fail.

Chances are, most people revert to survival mode.

That is not the mindset of a conqueror. To conquer is to venture into the unknown. There will be failures along the way, that's for sure. But with perseverance, a greater reward awaits the conqueror.

> "The thief does not come except to steal, and to kill, and to destroy. I have come that

they may have life, and that they may have it more abundantly."

John 10:10

Jesus came so that we do not only survive. He came so that we may thrive—which leads us to the next provision.

New wine

Wine has always been associated with celebration. In the Israelite culture, important events in the lives of people mean the sharing of wine. And new wine means a new reason to celebrate.

The very first miracle that Jesus performed involved wine. It was during a wedding feast in Cana. The celebration was well underway when the host suddenly ran out of wine. Running out of wine in such an occasion would bring disgrace to the groom. Thus, something had to be done.

> On the third day there was a wedding in Cana of Galilee, and the mother of Jesus was there. Now both Jesus and His disciples were invited to the wedding. And when they ran out of wine, the mother of Jesus said to Him, "They have no wine."

John 2:1-3

The rest of the narrative, as they say, is history. Jesus turned water into wine. And so, the celebration went on.

Even today, wine is central in festivities. So much so that a bottle of wine can cost hundreds or even thousands of pesos. And many of these festivities are to celebrate something new—the New Year, a new house, a new job, a new baby, and many others.

In the Philippines, people would go so far as to spend more than they can afford to celebrate. For celebrations often are synonymous to extravagance.

God's promise of new wine shows His extravagance in giving blessings. He did not just promise grain for sustenance, but also new wine for celebrations.

> Honor the LORD with your possessions, And with the firstfruits of all your increase; So your barns will be filled with plenty, And your vats will overflow with new wine.
>
> Proverbs 3:9-10

Oil

Oil is one of the elements used in the Tabernacle and, later, in the Temple. In many ways, it is the medium through which the Divine moves—especially in Old Testament times.

Remember that oil was the most commonly used material agent in the act of anointing. It was used to consecrate people and things for worship.

> Also Moses took the anointing oil, and anointed the tabernacle and all that was in it, and consecrated them. He sprinkled some of it on the altar seven times, anointed the altar and all its utensils, and the laver and its base, to consecrate them. And he poured some of the anointing oil on Aaron's head and anointed him, to consecrate him.
>
> Leviticus 8:10-12

Oil was also an ingredient in offerings to the LORD. It is usually sprinkled on or mixed with whatever is offered.

> And if you bring as an offering a grain offering baked in the oven, it shall be unleavened cakes of fine flour mixed with oil, or unleavened wafers anointed with oil.
>
> Leviticus 2:4

God provides us everything that we need—grain, new wine, and oil.

Grain, new wine, and oil—these are gifts from God for those who keep His words. Conversely, there is a price for disobedience and Scripture is explicit in what disobedience entails.

> You shall carry much seed out to the field but gather little in, for the locust shall consume it. You shall plant vineyards and tend them, but you shall neither drink of the wine nor gather the grapes; for the worms shall eat them. You shall have olive trees throughout all your territory, but you shall not anoint yourself with the oil; for your olives shall drop off.

> Deuteronomy 28:38-40

God gives and takes away. That is well within the scope of His sovereignty. Job, having lost everything but his life, fully understood this and even blessed the LORD for it.

> And he said: "Naked I came from my mother's womb, And naked shall I return there. The LORD gave, and the LORD has taken away; Blessed be the name of the LORD."

> Job 1:21

Moreover, grain, new wine, and oil are derived from plants. This means that the Promised Land would have lush vegetation. Vegetation means there would be several flowers and fruits. Flowers produce nectar. Bees collect nectar to produce honey.

God also promised to send grass in their fields for their livestock. The more grass for grazing, the bigger their herds and flocks would become. And these animals produce milk.

So, in essence, a land of hills and valleys becomes a land flowing with milk and honey because of God's provision.

What about us—modern-day Christians? What use do we have for grain, new wine, and oil? Surely, we use them in preparing food for our bodies. But what about food for our souls?

There is only one answer to that—Jesus.

Again, grain is the main ingredient of bread.

> And Jesus said to them, "I am the bread of life. He who comes to Me shall never hunger, and he who believes in Me shall never thirst."

> John 6:35

Jesus is the bread of life.

Wine is derived from the fruit of the vine.

> "I am the vine, you are the branches. He who abides in Me, and I in him, bears much fruit; for without Me you can do nothing."
>
> John 15:5

Jesus is the true vine.

In the introductory section of this book, we explored the account of Samuel anointing David to be the next king. The prophet anointed the shepherd boy with oil and something amazing happened: the Spirit of the LORD came upon David from that day forward.

Thus, the manifestation of anointing is the presence of the Spirit. And what did Jesus say about the Holy Spirit?

> "But the Helper, the Holy Spirit, whom the Father will send in My name, He will teach you all things, and bring to your remembrance all things that I said to you."
>
> John 14:26

If we confess to have received Jesus as our personal Lord and Savior, the Holy Spirit, whom the Father sent in Jesus' name, indwells in us.

Grain, new wine, and oil all point to Jesus.

> "Go therefore and make disciples of all the nations, baptizing them in the name of the Father and of the Son and of the Holy Spirit, teaching them to observe all things that I have commanded you; and lo, I am with you always, even to the end of the age." Amen."
>
> Matthew 28:19-20

God promised the conquerors grain, new wine, and oil in the Promised Land. Jesus promised us His presence.

> Yet in all these things we are more than conquerors through Him who loved us.
>
> Romans 8:37

In Jesus, we are more than conquerors!

THE SUCCESSION

This historical event happened right before the Israelites entered Canaan. God was giving them a heads up before they start their conquest. But equally important to conquering the land was conveying their personal experiences of God to their children.

> Therefore you shall love the LORD your God, and keep His charge, His statutes, His judgments, and His commandments always. Know today that I do not speak with your children, who have not known and who have not seen the chastening of the LORD your God, His greatness and His mighty hand and His outstretched arm—His signs and His acts which He did in the midst of Egypt, to Pharaoh king of Egypt, and to all his land...
>
> Deuteronomy 11:1-3

Recall that 40 years earlier, when the twelve spies were sent to evaluate the land, ten of them made disheartening reports of how high the walls of the cities and how big the giants in the land were. As a result, the people did not obey God. God's anger was again roused that He made the people roam the wilderness for 40 years—one year for every day the spies spent scouting the land. God also prohibited several of them, including Moses himself due to an earlier disobedience, from entering the Promised Land.

If all people aged 20 and above, except Caleb and Joshua, were to die in the wilderness, this means

God's message was for those who were able to witness God's wonders in Egypt and in the wilderness. Most of them were less than 60 years old when God spoke about the new land.

God's command was for them to pass on to the next generation what they had witnessed so that the next generation would have eye-witness accounts of what happened in Egypt and in the wilderness.

This is supplementary to an earlier command concerning the shema.

> And these words which I command you today shall be in your heart. You shall teach them diligently to your children, and shall talk of them when you sit in your house, when you walk by the way, when you lie down, and when you rise up.
>
> Deuteronomy 6:6-7

My grandmother on my father's side—the late Mrs. Paulita Castaño Ampong, from whom I was named— understood the "succession" command. After she retired from being a public school supervisor, she took it upon herself to organize the many evangelical Christian denominations in our small town to teach the Gospel and Christian values to pupils in public schools. Pupils with evangelical

Christian parents from each grade level were gathered together in one classroom to hear Bible stories and other Christian teachings for about 30 minutes every Monday morning.

She knew Scripture and the importance of imparting it to the next generation.

As combatants in the Great War, the command to teach diligently to our children His goodness and greatness applies to us. His grace behooves us to share what we know and what we have witnessed to the next generation. This is what succession means in God's Army.

Let's not fear to conquer new ground. God has promised us to provide everything that we need—grain, new wine, and oil. And every time we conquer new ground by the grace of God, let us tell our story to others so that they would come to know His goodness, greatness, and grace.

THE GENERAL

JOSHUA 8

The general is the top leader of the military. As such, he is the commander of the entire army. In the Philippine setup, the Chief of Staff of the Armed Forces is the highest-ranking officer—he is the top general. He answers to the Commander-in-Chief—the president of the country.

The Battle of Cannae in 216 BC is considered to be one of the greatest in history. Despite being outnumbered by the Roman troops, Hannibal led the Carthaginian army to victory. Taking advantage of the terrain, he forced the Romans to take a narrow and deep formation; the Carthaginians took a crescent formation with the cavalry on the flanks. As the Roman troops pushed forward, the center of Hannibal's army gradually retreated but did not break formation. The superior Carthaginian cavalry overpowered their foes and pushed further forward eventually making the crescent formation into a circle—thus enveloping the Roman army from the flanks. Military historians would later refer to the battle as "as a classic example of a victorious double envelopment.[9]"

Although the Carthaginians were later defeated by the Romans, the Battle of Cannae cemented Hannibal's legacy as one of the greatest military leaders of all time.

I know of a better battle and a better military leader. Centuries earlier, Joshua and the Israelites also used strategy to defeat an enemy army. The narrative is found in Joshua 8.

THE DIRECTIVE

What set Joshua apart as a great military leader was that his directive to his men came from God Himself—the Commander-in-Chief of commanders-in-chief. The men of war were under his command; he was under God's command.

The directive had three parts: an internal preparatory command, a physical preparatory command and a command to take action.

---

[9] https://www.britannica.com/event/Battle-of-Cannae

Now the LORD said to Joshua: "Do not be afraid, nor be dismayed; take all the people of war with you, and arise, go up to Ai. See, I have given into your hand the king of Ai, his people, his city, and his land. And you shall do to Ai and its king as you did to Jericho and its king. Only its spoil and its cattle you shall take as booty for yourselves. Lay an ambush for the city behind it."

Joshua 8:1-2

Do not be afraid, nor be dismayed

God started by saying, "Do not be afraid, nor be dismayed." This is a gentle reminder of what God had said to Joshua and the people as they were entering the land.

Have I not commanded you? Be strong and of good courage; do not be afraid, nor be dismayed, for the LORD your God is with you wherever you go.

Joshua 1:9

These words are repeated several times in the Book of Joshua. Almost always they start with "be strong and of good courage."

At first glance, the command, "Be strong and of good courage; do not be afraid, nor be dismayed" sounds like what the commander of an army would typically say to his troops before a battle to encourage his men to do their best. But this command goes beyond being strong and brave for war. It is for a greater battle—the Great War. Earlier in Joshua 1, God said:

> Only be strong and very courageous, that you may observe to do according to all the law which Moses My servant commanded you; do not turn from it to the right hand or to the left, that you may prosper wherever you go.
>
> Joshua 1:7

The command was more for internal strength and courage to follow the law He gave through Moses. As what we can read in the Book of Joshua, the Israelites were able to conquer much of the land. Thus, they did well in being strong and courageous for war. However, much of their failures were from being unable to be strong and courageous enough to obey God.

When I started to run regularly, I did not immediately buy new shoes and outfits. I decided to prepare internally rather than externally. First, I started with brisk walks on the treadmill for about 20 minutes. Gradually, I increased the duration and the speed. After about a month on the treadmill, I decided to run outdoors. All the while, I was using an old pair of shoes (which were not even for running or training) and my existing clothes.

Somehow, I realized early on that I had to develop the habit of running regularly first. It was only after I developed the discipline, and after my old shoes were worn out, that I bought a pair of running shoes. My wife also bought me a shirt and a pair of shorts that are for running and training.

The army had to prepare internally. Being obedient to God takes a lot of strength and courage.

Take all the people of war… , arise, go up to Ai

After the command to prepare internally came the second part of the directive which was the physical preparatory command. It had three facets. First, it's a command to take all the people of war into the battlefield. This is huge. It tells us at least two things: that everyone should be in the fray and that we should not take the enemy lightly.

In the spiritual warfare we are in, everyone who is on the side of truth should join the battle—everyone should do his part no matter how small. The enemy knows that he loses in the end that is why he is desperate to win in the skirmishes—he will not go easy on us. That is why we should go into battle with every combatant we have in the army. Yes, we will win the war in the end; but we should also win each and every battle.

> Or else, if indeed you do go back, and cling to the remnant of these nations—these that remain among you—and make marriages with them, and go in to them and they to you, know for certain that the LORD your God will no longer drive out these nations from before you. But they shall be snares and traps to you, and scourges on your sides and thorns in your eyes, until you perish from this good land which the LORD your God has given you.
>
> Joshua 23:12-13

The Israelites conquered much of the land but not all—they won the war but not all battles. That is why they were not able to drive out all inhabitants of the land. And these people became snares and traps to them.

The main text for this chapter tells of the people's second attack against Ai. There was a prior attempt to attack the city. Fresh from their spectacular victory over Jericho, Joshua sent out spies to Ai. His men reported back that there were so few men in Ai.

> And they returned to Joshua and said to him, "Do not let all the people go up, but let about two or three thousand men go up and attack

> Ai. Do not weary all the people there, for the people of Ai are few." So about three thousand men went up there from the people, but they fled before the men of Ai.
>
> Joshua 7:3-4

It was either they underestimated the enemy or they were overconfident. Regardless, they were defeated. However, there was a deeper reason for this defeat—which will be tackled later in this chapter.

That is why God was specific the second time around. He commanded that all people of war should go up to Ai. He wanted the people to go full throttle on the attack and not take the enemy lightly.

The second part of the preparatory command was just one word—arise. But the Hebrew verb holds more meaning than the English translation. The original Hebrew verb that means "to arise" has a very militaristic implication. It is equivalent to the military command "attention."

It's not enough for the people to be internally prepared. They also needed to be physically alert. Their siege on the enemy would later become one of the most strategically executed attacks during the years of conquest. Every soldier in the army had to be alert because each one plays an important role in the organization.

To arise is to be alert. In war, officers give out instructions or signals in the middle of the battle. Missing out on these instructions could potentially be detrimental to the strategy—no matter how brilliant it may be.

> Then the LORD said to Joshua, "Stretch out the spear that is in your hand toward Ai, for I will give it into your hand." And Joshua stretched out the spear that was in his hand toward the city. So those in ambush arose quickly out of their place; they ran as soon as he had stretched out his hand, and they entered the city and took it, and hurried to set the city on fire. And when the men of Ai looked behind them, they saw, and behold, the smoke of the city ascended to heaven. So they had no power to flee this way or that way, and the people who had fled to the wilderness turned back on the pursuers. Now when Joshua and all Israel saw that the ambush had taken the city and that the smoke of the city ascended, they turned back and struck down the men of Ai. Then the others came out of the city against them; so they were caught in the midst of Israel, some on this side and some on that side. And

they struck them down, so that they let none of them remain or escape.

Joshua 8:18-22

Third, the command specified the place to where God was sending the army. God was sending them back to the place where they tasted defeat in the Promised Land. It was their first defeat after their victory over Jericho. But, technically, it was not their first defeat in the Promised Land. Forty years earlier, they were rounded up by the enemy after they refused to conquer the land. The "where" is important because it's integral to God's promise.

"Also I give to you and your descendants after you the land in which you are a stranger, **all the land of Canaan**, as an everlasting possession; and I will be their God."

Genesis 17:8; emphasis mine

Ai was within the Promised Land—something that God has promised to Abraham and his descendants. It had to be conquered like the rest of the cities and settlements in Canaan.

God does not give in half measures. When He promises something, He gives all of it. Maybe not all at the same time, but all, nonetheless. He does not hold back.

> He who did not spare His own Son, but delivered Him up for us all, how shall He not with Him also freely give us all things?
>
> Romans 8:32

Do to Ai... as you did Jericho...

The third part of the directive was the command to take action. This too was given in three facets. The first one was a command to see the outcome of the battle before it even started. If it were from a human being, it would have sounded arrogant. But coming from God Himself, it was an affirmation of His promise to give the land to the people.

> Every place that the sole of your foot will tread upon I have given you, as I said to Moses.
>
> Joshua 1:3

Before they conquered Jericho, God had also promised them victory.

> And the LORD said to Joshua: "See! I have given Jericho into your hand, its king, and the mighty men of valor."
>
> Joshua 6:2

Isn't it a beautiful thing that the Commander-in-Chief has already promised the outcome even before the battle started? All Christians are part of the Army of God but many choose to be silent and complacent because they fail to see the favorable outcome in the future.

The Book of Revelation is an account of future events where we, those who are on the side of truth, emerge victorious in the Great War as we welcome the second coming of Jesus! This is what most combatants of this war forget or fail to see. But if the account recorded in Joshua is an indication, seeing that outcome, even before the battle starts, is an imperative.

Next came the "what" of the command to take action. God commanded the people to do to Ai what they did to Jericho, which was to utterly destroy the city and its inhabitants. They were only to take the spoils and the livestock—no prisoners.

It is also a command to remember a past victory. The circumstances and the methods of conquest may be different from before but what they were commanded to look back *to* was the victory—the outcome that was already promised.

Further, it is a command to destroy the past sins committed by the inhabitants of the land. The original inhabitants worshipped and offered sacrifices to the baals—practices that are an abomination to God.

> "When you come into the land which the Lord your God is giving you, you shall not learn to follow the abominations of those nations.

> "For all who do these things are an abomination to the Lord, and because of these abominations the Lord your God drives them out from before you."

> Deuteronomy 18:9, 12

The final part of the command to take action is the "how." God provided the scheme with which the people were to achieve their goal. And it was to set an ambush behind the city.

Thus, God gave a directive with many layers. Still, He left room for Joshua and the people to exercise free will. And this is where God's plans work in harmony with human abilities through obedience.

THE STRATEGY

In His directive, God provided the general scheme of the operation. It was Joshua, the leader, who strategized their attack based on God's plan.

So he took about five thousand men and set them in ambush between Bethel and Ai, on the west side of the city. And when they had set the people, all the army that was on the north of the city, and its rear guard on the west of the city, Joshua went that night into the midst of the valley.

Joshua 8:12-13

Joshua sent 5,000 men behind the city, on the west side, to lay in ambush. The main army was stationed on the north of the city. Joshua stayed with the main troops. The Israelite army was 30,000 strong against Ai's 12,000.

Joshua stationed the main troops such that the people of Ai could see them while the ambush secretly hid behind the city. The main troops would engage Ai in battle in the valley. The Israelites would then act as if they were on retreat. This would have the people of Ai believing they were winning again. Ai would pursue the main troops leaving the city defenseless. The ambush team would then attack the city and burn it.

The main troops would then turn around to attack the pursuing enemy. The ambush team would come out of the city and attack the enemy in the battlefield field. Thus, the enemy was caught between attacking troops. All 12,000 fighting men of Ai were struck with the sword that day. And the Israelites laid waste to the city, only taking the spoils and the livestock.

In life and in ministry, God shows us a vision—a clear vision of the future. But He also leaves room for our God-given skills and talents to be used to achieve that goal.

This is why any organization, Christian or otherwise, always has one top leader. This is not so he or she can lord it over the people. It is so that he can execute God's plans. This is the job of the general—the top leader.

There are of course instances in the Bible where God gave very specific instructions on how things are to be done. Like the details of the Tabernacle and the rituals to be performed in it. The same is true when He commissioned the building of the ark. More so, in God's plan of salvation for all. In all these times when God gave specifics, still He used humans to achieve His goals. God gave the design specifications of the Tabernacle to Moses; He instructed Noah on how to build the Ark; He sent His only begotten Son, Jesus, to die for the sins of all.

THE COMPLIANCE

Yes, God gave the directive which Joshua, the leader, passed onto the people. Their obedience to the directive gave them the upper hand in the ensuing battle. But what really sealed the deal was their compliance to an earlier, overarching command.

When they were about to attack Jericho, a command was given to destroy the city and everything in it.

> The city and all that is in it shall be devoted to the LORD for destruction. Only Rahab the prostitute and all who are with her in her house shall live because she hid the messengers we sent. As for you, keep away from the things devoted to destruction, so as not to covet and take any of the devoted things and make the camp of Israel an object for destruction, bringing trouble upon it. But all silver and gold, and vessels of bronze and iron, are sacred to the LORD; they shall go into the treasury of the LORD.
>
> Joshua 6:17-19 NRSV

Thus they destroyed everything by the edge of the sword.

> Then they devoted to destruction by the edge of the sword all in the city, both men and women, young and old, oxen, sheep, and donkeys.
>
> Joshua 6:21 NRSV

Or so they thought.

Remember the Israelites were defeated on their first attempt to conquer Ai. It was because one of them did not comply with the command to destroy everything in Jericho and gave in to personal desires.

> Israel has sinned; they have transgressed my covenant that I imposed on them. They have taken some of the devoted things; they have stolen, they have acted deceitfully, and they have put them among their own belongings. Therefore the Israelites are unable to stand before their enemies; they turn their backs to their enemies, because they have become a thing devoted for destruction themselves. I will be with you no more, unless you destroy the devoted things from among you.
>
> Joshua 7:11-12 NRSV

Because of the noncompliance of one, the entire army suffered.

The second time around, the Israelites complied with God's command. (Unlike in Jericho, they were permitted to take the livestock.)

> When Israel had finished slaughtering all the inhabitants of Ai in the open wilderness

where they pursued them, and when all of them to the very last had fallen by the edge of the sword, all Israel returned to Ai, and attacked it with the edge of the sword.

Only the livestock and the spoil of that city Israel took as their booty, according to the word of the LORD that he had issued to Joshua. So Joshua burned Ai, and made it forever a heap of ruins, as it is to this day.

Joshua 8:24, 27-28 NRSV

A good leader is indeed a good follower. Joshua was that kind of leader—one who obeyed God.

God gives the directive. Our obedience to the directive is not to curtail human creativity and strategy. It is to show that if we have surrendered all to God, He ultimately gives us the victory.

THE SPECIAL OPERATIVE

JUDGES 3:12-30

Special operatives or special forces are "specially designated, organized, selected, trained, and equipped forces using unconventional techniques and modes of employment."[10] These operatives conduct military activities which may include counterterrorism and unconventional warfare.

The 2013 Academy Awards Best Motion Picture movie "Argo" was based on a true story of a CIA (America's Central Intelligence Agency) agent who dared to rescue six American citizens in Tehran during the hostage crisis in the U.S. Embassy in Iran in 1979. The agent—technically a special operative

---

10 https://en.wikipedia.org/wiki/Special_operations

—went into hostile territory in the guise of a Hollywood movie producer scouting for a location of a film. As the movie tagline goes "The movie was fake. The mission was real."[11]

The main passage for this chapter tells of Ehud, one of the "minor judges" of Israel after the years of conquest. The term "minor judges," like "minor prophets," does not mean their contribution to the history of Israel is any less significant. The term "minor judges" simply means there's not much written about them in the book of Judges (unlike Samson or Gideon whose stories span several chapters).

The unconventional warfare that Ehud contributed to history was assassination. He may be the only assassin whose feat was recorded in the pages of the Bible. Assassination involves the discreet killing of a high-profile person for a cause—usually political or religious in nature.

Let's set things straight: premeditated murder is prohibited. It's one of the Ten Commandments.

"You shall not murder."

Exodus 20:13

---

11 https://www.imdb.com/title/tt1024648/?ref_=fn_al_tt_1

But many people, including professing Christians, find it hard to fathom that a good God would allow the killing of thousands—especially in Old Testament times.

To address this, let's go back to one of the underlying points in this book—God has relegated dominion of the world to mankind. That is why when He goes into action, He would always use human beings. We already explored the lives of a number of them. And the epitome of God's human instrument is Jesus Himself.

Jesus had to come in human form so that God could take action through Him. He even allowed Himself to be subject to human judicial ways and practices when He went to trial on His way to the cross.

Secondly, the deaths that God "allowed" in the Old Testament were a result of the people's direct affront against Him.

> "When you come into the land which the LORD your God is giving you, you shall not learn to follow the abominations of those nations. There shall not be found among you anyone who makes his son or his daughter pass through the fire, or one who practices witchcraft, or a soothsayer, or one who interprets omens, or a sorcerer, or one who

conjures spells, or a medium, or a spiritist, or one who calls up the dead. For all who do these things are an abomination to the LORD, and because of these abominations the LORD your God drives them out from before you. You shall be blameless before the LORD your God."

Deuteronomy 18:9-13

In order to implement His judgment upon people and nations that practice abominable or repulsive acts, God will have to act through humans. He already gave the mandate to man on the sixth day of creation.

Ehud was one of the first judges of Israel. His call came when the people of Israel were oppressed by the king of the Moabites.

> And the children of Israel again did evil in the sight of the LORD. So the LORD strengthened Eglon king of Moab against Israel, because they had done evil in the sight of the LORD. Then he gathered to himself the people of Ammon and Amalek, went and defeated Israel, and took possession of the City of Palms. So the children of Israel served Eglon king of Moab eighteen years.

> Judges 3:12-14

It may be said that the Moabites, Ammonites, and Amalekites were not Canaanites—they were not part of the people to be conquered. But they had deep history with the Israelites. The Moabites and Ammonites were descendants of Lot—Abraham's nephew. These people were born out of incest when Lot's daughters had sons by their father after the fall of Sodom and Gomorrah.

> Thus both the daughters of Lot were with child by their father. The firstborn bore a son and called his name Moab; he is the father of the Moabites to this day. And the younger, she also bore a son and called his name Ben-Ammi; he is the father of the people of Ammon to this day.
>
> Genesis 19:36-38

They were a product of abominable acts before God. To make matters worse for themselves, these people refused safe passage for the Israelites when they were on their way to the Promised Land. These people also sacrificed their children to their gods—again, an abomination in the sight of God. That's a triple whammy right there. These sins resulted to the prohibition of Ammonites or Moabites from the assembly of the LORD.

> "An Ammonite or Moabite shall not enter the assembly of the LORD; even to the tenth

generation none of his descendants shall enter the assembly of the LORD forever, because they did not meet you with bread and water on the road when you came out of Egypt, and because they hired against you Balaam the son of Beor from Pethor of Mesopotamia, to curse you."

Deuteronomy 23:3-4

The Amalekites, on the other hand, were the first people to attack the Israelites soon after they left Egypt. That is why when Israel finally had a king, one of God's first directives was to destroy the Amalekites.

Thus says the LORD of hosts: 'I will punish Amalek for what he did to Israel, how he ambushed him on the way when he came up from Egypt. Now go and attack Amalek, and utterly destroy all that they have, and do not spare them. But kill both man and woman, infant and nursing child, ox and sheep, camel and donkey.'

I Samuel 15:2-3

Back to our main text: God raised up Ehud.

But when the children of Israel cried out to the LORD, the LORD raised up a deliverer for them: Ehud the son of Gera, the Benjamite, a left-handed man. By him the children of Israel sent tribute to Eglon king of Moab. Now Ehud made himself a dagger (it was double-edged and a cubit in length) and fastened it under his clothes on his right thigh. So he brought the tribute to Eglon king of Moab. (Now Eglon was a very fat man.) And when he had finished presenting the tribute, he sent away the people who had carried the tribute. But he himself turned back from the stone images that were at Gilgal, and said, "I have a secret message for you, O king." He said, "Keep silence!" And all who attended him went out from him. So Ehud came to him (now he was sitting upstairs in his cool private chamber). Then Ehud said, "I have a message from God for you." So he arose from his seat. Then Ehud reached with his left hand, took the dagger from his right thigh, and thrust it into his belly. Even the hilt went in after the blade, and the fat closed over the blade, for he did not draw the dagger out of his belly; and his entrails came out. Then Ehud went out through the porch and shut the doors of the upper room behind him and locked them.

Judges 3:15-23

The story of Ehud may not be as popular as other stories but we can definitely learn from it.

THE 'HANDICAP'

With only an estimated 10% of the population being left-handed, we could say that we live in a right-handed world. Even modern science still could not fully explain the factors behind left-handedness.

Throughout the course of history, cultures, as reflected in language, have associated "left" with bad or wrong. For example, the Old French of "left" is "sinistre," which is from the Latin word "sinister" which means "left." This somehow survived in the Italian "sinistra," which means "left." In modern English, "sinister" means something harmful or evil.

The writer of Judges may have been familiar with the rarity of left-handed people that he specifically included this detail in the passage. Many readers would naturally consider this as a handicap on the part of Ehud.

By definition, a handicap is something—a circumstance or condition—that restricts or hinders progress or success. It is something that puts someone at a disadvantage.

> Let no one deceive himself. If anyone among you seems to be wise in this age, let him

become a fool that he may become wise. For the wisdom of this world is foolishness with God. For it is written, "He catches the wise in their own craftiness"

I Corinthians 3:18-19

As we have come to learn, God's wisdom is far above ours. What many of us see as a handicap could be used to accomplish His purpose and give glory to His name.

Right-handed people would normally strap their weapons onto their left thigh. So Ehud did the opposite—he strapped and concealed his dagger onto his right thigh. What seemed like his *handicap* handicapped the guards of the enemy.

God used his "handicap" and the lack of diligence of the guards to deliver a fatal blow to the enemy. The guards may have been used to checking the left thigh for concealed weapons only. They did not bother checking his right thigh.

In life and in ministry, people almost always define others by their handicap. And this is not just limited to physical disabilities.

What many of us are very familiar with is the handicap of youth. Growing up, we usually get discouraged to try something new. Our youth, our lack of experience, becomes our handicap. The Apostle Paul was aware of this as he was training Timothy up. He knew that because Timothy was still young, people might look down on him. So Paul wrote to Timothy about this.

> Let no one despise your youth, but be an example to the believers in word, in conduct, in love, in spirit, in faith, in purity. Till I come, give attention to reading, to exhortation, to doctrine. Do not neglect the gift that is in you, which was given to you by prophecy with the laying on of the hands of the eldership. Meditate on these things; give yourself entirely to them, that your progress may be evident to all.

> I Timothy 4:12-15

Paul instructed Timothy to immerse himself into reading Scripture and to hone his gift so that his progress would become evident. Timothy couldn't do anything with his youth—he couldn't accelerate his aging. He can only accelerate his learning and his growth in wisdom.

I have already shared that I had been diagnosed with a rare critical illness. Because of it, my neurologist advised me to not work a regular job anymore. I took the advice. I resigned.

This gave me plenty of time to read the Bible and reflect on God's Word. Eventually, I was able to write this book.

It was also during the time after I quit my job that God blessed me and my wife with a baby boy. I have been a full time dad ever since he was born.

Through my "handicap," God has given me breakthroughs!

THE 'PROPER' CHANNEL

In the world, there are established orders that make societies run. Like when selecting a national leader, depending on the type of government, there are laws that make sure the proper process is observed. And there are similar laws concerning the other components of society.

The Apostle Paul emphasized that governing authorities are part of God's intricate design.

> Let every soul be subject to the governing authorities. For there is no authority except from God, and the authorities that exist are appointed by God. Therefore whoever resists the authority resists the ordinance of God, and those who resist will bring judgment on themselves. For rulers are not a terror to good works, but to evil. Do you want to be

unafraid of the authority? Do what is good, and you will have praise from the same. For he is God's minister to you for good. But if you do evil, be afraid; for he does not bear the sword in vain; for he is God's minister, an avenger to execute wrath on him who practices evil.

Romans 13:1-4

People do not always welcome social orders—especially if these orders are imposed on them. Such was the case of the Israelites during the time of Ehud. They were under the oppressive rule of the king of the Moabites. Most probably, much of their freedom was curtailed and they could hardly act on their own accord.

According to the passage in Judges, God raised up a deliverer when the children of Israel prayed. So, God gave the people Ehud. All they needed was to strike a big blow onto the enemy.

The Israelites may have been aware that the biggest blow that they could inflict onto the enemy was through the king of Moab. And *that* may be easier said than done. As the king of an invading nation, Eglon may have been heavily guarded. And he should be, because a few decades earlier, the people of Moab have seen and heard of the conquest of the Israelites. This time around they were just an instrument to punish the erring children of Israel.

So, how would the deliverer approach the king of Moab? They used the proper channel.

Being under the rule of Moab, the Israelites and other conquered people were to present tributes to Eglon. This was the proper channel they used to get close to the target.

Established orders in society may be birthed by human minds—some of them may not be exactly what God would have wanted. Nonetheless, they could still be used by God to deliver His message, blessing, or judgment. At the very least, these channels can present an opportunity for God's purpose.

> "But beware! For you will be handed over to the courts and will be flogged with whips in the synagogues. You will stand trial before governors and kings because you are my followers. But this will be your opportunity to tell the rulers and other unbelievers about me."
>
> Matthew 10:17-18 NLT

When Jesus was about to send out His disciples, He forewarned them that they will be arrested. But He also told them that it will be an opportunity for them to tell people about Him.

THE FOLLOWTHROUGH

The assassination of Eglon was only the initial blow to the enemy. It would have been for naught if the action ended there. After Ehud delivered a fatal blow to the head of the enemy, he rallied his people and led them.

> And it happened, when he arrived, that he blew the trumpet in the mountains of Ephraim, and the children of Israel went down with him from the mountains; and he led them. Then he said to them, "Follow me, for the LORD has delivered your enemies the Moabites into your hand." So they went down after him, seized the fords of the Jordan leading to Moab, and did not allow anyone to cross over. And at that time they killed about ten thousand men of Moab, all stout men of valor; not a man escaped.
>
> Judges 3:27-29

As recorded in Judges 3, it is said that the enemy "defeated Israel, and took possession of the City of Palms." The City of Palms refers to Jericho—the first city that the Israelites conquered.

It may have been that within those 18 years when Israel served Eglon king of Moab, the Moabites and their allies were also trying to expand their conquest. Jericho may have been their garrison in the land of Canaan, which was west of the Jordan; Moab was located east of the Jordan. The enemy troops may have occupied Jericho and stationed soldiers there—making the city their portal into the rest of the land.

Lead the main troops

Eglon may have been in his palace in Moab when Ehud assassinated him. After delivering the blow, Ehud escaped back to Canaan and rallied the people in the territory of Ephraim—which is north of Jericho; Moab was located southeast. He then led the people.

The people's advance, with the leadership of Ehud, made sure of their victory—it was the necessary followthrough after the initial blow.

About a decade ago, I was part of a creative team in UCCP Bradford Church[12] who set out to make a commemorative coffee table book as part of the centennial celebration of the dedication of the original church building. The team was composed of dedicated individuals with different gifts fit to

---

[12] Bradford Church is my UCCP (United Church of Christ in the Philippines) home church away from my hometown

make the project work. We had an opening salvo where we presented the proposed contents as well as the sample layouts of the spreads. In short, we delivered an amazing first blow.

However, the project never materialized. Sure, the enemy may have had a hand in it. But in hindsight, I think the reason why the project failed was because the creative team was not able to followthrough; we were not able to rally the congregation—the main troops—behind us.

The assassination without the main troops is an incomplete move.

Stop the problem at the source

Although not stated in the passage, the main troops' first action may have been to liberate Jericho from the enemy soldiers stationed in the city. Then they "seized the fords[13] of the Jordan leading to Moab." These fords may have been around the same place where the Israelites crossed when they first came into the land.

Retaking Jericho would mean that the Moabites and their allies would need reinforcement from their land. That was why Ehud and the Israelites seized the fords of the Jordan—to cut off the supply of

---

[13] Fords are shallow segments of a river or stream where one can wade through to cross to the other side.

enemy soldiers from east of the river. In the passage, the Israelites killed 10,000 men from Moab at the fords. Imagine how much damage 10,000 men of valor can inflict onto Israel.

Many times in our life we experience recurring problems simply because we fail to cut them off at the source.

As an environmental planning consultant, I help organizations comply with environmental requirements of their projects. In a recent project, I helped a school in complying with American environmental standards for a building they were erecting. The engagement involved coordinating with the termite control service provider to ensure that they also comply with the standards.

I had learned that the most important part of termite control is finding and destroying the nest and killing the queen. If not killed, the queen will just keep on spawning termites, and the problem will persist. The wooden components of the building will periodically be eaten away by the termites and will have to be repaired or replaced over and over again.

Getting rid of the termite queen is cutting off the problem at the source.

The assassination was just the first blow. No matter how explosive the first blow may have been, the followthrough carries the bulk of the mission through to the end. Oftentimes, this requires cutting off the problem at the source.

Bask in the aftermath

God raised Ehud up after the Israelites suffered for 18 years under the Moabites.

> So Moab was subdued that day under the hand of Israel. And the land had rest for eighty years.
>
> Judges 3:30

Through one man, God's deliverance came to the people and they had rest for 80 years!

The 18 years of suffering under the Moabites were a result of Israel's disobedience. Those 18 years were but a moment. Many of those who were born during the occupation of the Moabites lived to see the day of God's deliverance. Just as the Psalmist David declared:

> For His anger is but for a moment, His favor is for life; Weeping may endure for a night, But joy comes in the morning.
>
> Psalms 30:5

The aftermath of the battle was rest for 80 years. And that is more than three generations. This means that those who witnessed God's deliverance in the time of Ehud lived to tell the story to their grandchildren without threats from the enemy.

When Adam sinned, sin entered the world. Adam's sin brought death, so death spread to everyone, for everyone sinned. Yes, people sinned even before the law was given. But it was not counted as sin because there was not yet any law to break. Still, everyone died— from the time of Adam to the time of Moses— even those who did not disobey an explicit commandment of God, as Adam did. Now Adam is a symbol, a representation of Christ, who was yet to come. But there is a great difference between Adam's sin and God's gracious gift. For the sin of this one man, Adam, brought death to many. But even greater is God's wonderful grace and his gift of forgiveness to many through this other man, Jesus Christ. And the result of God's gracious gift is very different from the result of that one man's sin. For Adam's sin led to condemnation, but God's free gift leads to our being made right with God, even though we are guilty of many sins. For the sin of this one man, Adam, caused death to rule over many. But even greater is God's wonderful grace and his gift of righteousness, for all who receive it will live in triumph over sin and death through this one man, Jesus Christ.

Romans 5:12-17 NLT

Through one Man, there is deliverance from sin and death. We may suffer under the oppression of sin on earth, but when we believe in the saving grace of God through Jesus Christ, we can bask in a place with golden streets for eternity!

> The twelve gates were twelve pearls: each individual gate was of one pearl. And the street of the city was pure gold, like transparent glass.
>
> Revelation 21:21

As I personally experienced, our "handicaps" can be God's channels to do great things. Let's use them to achieve the purpose God has set for us. But an initial blow—no matter how explosive—is not enough. We need to do the necessary followthrough works to finish the job.

THE ENGINEERING UNIT

NEHEMIAH 4

The military engineering unit is primarily tasked to build and maintain military transport and communication lines. Members of the unit build fortifications, roads, bridges, airfields, ports, and hospitals, especially in hostile environments.

The Battle of Normandy would go down in history as the beginning of the end of World War II. On June 6, 1944, the Allied Forces (U.S., British and Canadian forces) launched simultaneous landings on five (5) beachheads in Normandy, France.

The forces—mostly composed of newly drafted servicemen—had to fight through an array of defensive installations to secure the beach. They had to go through log posts (vertically erected logs; some with mines) and hedgehogs (barricades made out of three crossed steel beams about 1.5 meter tall), and other obstacles. The soldiers made their advance while trying to survive enemy attack from bunkers on top of the hills behind the beach.

The invasion in Normandy took years of planning. The Allied Forces knew that the beach would be heavily fortified. Taking the beach would be difficult. But it had to be done in order to win the war. France was eventually liberated from the Nazi after about three months.

Defense forces always have the advantage of fortification. The Allied invasion of Normandy may have been a success but not without the loss of thousands. The military engineering unit of the Nazi did their job well but not well enough.

Such is the value of fortification and the efforts of the engineering unit that builds it.

About four centuries before the birth of Jesus, ex-exiles from Babylon started to rebuild the wall of Jerusalem. Remember that the Israelites were in exile for 70 years as a result of the capture of Jerusalem by King Nebuchadnezzar of Babylon.

In the third year of the reign of Jehoiakim king of Judah, Nebuchadnezzar king of Babylon came to Jerusalem and besieged it. And the LORD gave Jehoiakim king of Judah into his hand, with some of the articles of the house of God, which he carried into the land of Shinar to the house of his god; and he brought the articles into the treasure house of his god.

Daniel 1:1-2

Israel's exile was permitted by God because of their continual sinning. But this chapter is not about that.

The events in Nehemiah 4 happened after earlier batches of ex-exiles had already returned to Jerusalem. The people were in deep sorrow because the walls and the city itself had lain in ruins for several years. With Nehemiah as their leader, the people started to rebuild the walls of the city.

THE ENEMY'S PLOT

We have already established the existence of the Great War and that there is a great divide between the two sides. We are on the side of light, truth, and life; the enemy brings darkness, falsehood, and death.

Combatants on the side of good often become complacent. It has been said that the greatest lie the devil—the enemy—has told the world is that evil does not exist. Acknowledging that there is an enemy will do our army good. And the enemy will do everything to pull anyone and everyone to the side of darkness.

But what does the enemy do? Having knowledge of the ways and plots of the enemy will give us the upper hand in this war.

When the first batch of ex-exiles returned from Babylon after 70 years in exile, other people have already occupied the areas around Jerusalem. At this point in history, they personified the enemy.

> But it so happened, when Sanballat heard that we were rebuilding the wall, that he was furious and very indignant, and mocked the Jews. And he spoke before his brethren and the army of Samaria, and said, "What are these feeble Jews doing? Will they fortify themselves? Will they offer sacrifices? Will they complete it in a day? Will they revive the stones from the heaps of rubbish—stones that are burned?"
>
> Nehemiah 4:1-2

Deny our strength

In *The Warrior*, we learned how the Israelite army let the enemy define the terms of battle. This made them fear the enemy. This made them lose the battle before it even began.

The enemy army wanted to define the terms of battle because they knew that if they were to fight army-to-army, the Israelites may have a better chance of winning. So they played to their strength —a one-on-one battle with their giant of a champion. In other words, the enemy denied the strength of the people of God.

In the Nehemiah 4, Sanballat described the Jews as "feeble." Someone feeble is someone who lacks the necessary strength to accomplish something.

Not much is written about Sanballat. But we can safely assume *what* he was thinking when he called the Jews "feeble." For one thing, he likely knew that the Jews had been a defeated people. The people of the Southern Kingdom of Judah had been defeated by Nebuchadnezzar and were exiled to Babylon. While in Babylon, the Babylonian Empire was overthrown by the Persian Empire. In essence, the Jews had been defeated twice.

The prophet Jeremiah wrote about the affliction of the Jews in exile.

My soul has been cast far away from peace; I have forgotten happiness. So I say, "My strength has perished And so has my hope and expectation from the LORD." Remember [O LORD] my affliction and my wandering, the wormwood and the gall (bitterness). My soul continually remembers them And is bowed down within me. But this I call to mind, Therefore I have hope. It is because of the LORD's lovingkindnesses that we are not consumed, Because His [tender] compassions never fail. They are new every morning; Great and beyond measure is Your faithfulness.

Lamentations 3:17-23 AMP

The life of the Jews in exile would later be mirrored by the persecution of the early Christians.

We are hard-pressed on every side, yet not crushed; we are perplexed, but not in despair; persecuted, but not forsaken; struck down, but not destroyed...

II Corinthians 4:8-9

It would seem that the enemy has been working tirelessly throughout history. Jesus described how the enemy works in the Parable of the Wheat and the Tares.

Another parable He put forth to them, saying: "The kingdom of heaven is like a man who sowed good seed in his field; but while men slept, his enemy came and sowed tares among the wheat and went his way. But when the grain had sprouted and produced a crop, then the tares also appeared."

Matthew 13:24-26

The enemy comes at night to sow discontent, lies, and troubles.

When we decided to follow Jesus, He never promised a life without trials. In fact He warned us that we will have troubles in the world.

"These things I have spoken to you, that in Me you may have peace. In the world you will have tribulation; but be of good cheer, I have overcome the world."

John 16:33

When we feel weary like the exiles or the early Christians, it may be a product poor decisions, but we should not disregard the work of the enemy. It is him trying to make us forget that Jesus has already overcome the world and all its troubles. It is him denying our strength yet again. Yes, we are weak if we rely on our own strength, but we derive our strength from Jesus, just as the Old Testament Jews drew strength from the LORD.

> I can do all things through Christ who strengthens me.

> Philippians 4:13

Undermine our objective

When the ex-exiles—the builders of the wall—came back to Jerusalem, they had one objective: rebuild the walls of the city. The broken wall was a physical representation of how broken they were as a people.

> And they said to me, "The survivors who are left from the captivity in the province are there in great distress and reproach. The wall of Jerusalem is also broken down, and its gates are burned with fire."

> Nehemiah 1:3

Without walls, the city was defenseless. It was susceptible to enemy attacks. It was a matter of national security that they rebuild their first line of defense. It made sense that rebuilding the walls was their primary objective.

In the time after the Exodus, after the people met Him in Mt. Sinai, God commanded the people to spy out the Promised Land before they conquer it. To spy out is to learn more about something by making careful observations.

> And the LORD spoke to Moses, saying, "Send men to spy out the land of Canaan, which I am giving to the children of Israel; from each tribe of their fathers you shall send a man, every one a leader among them."

> Numbers 13:1-2

Why would God issue such a command if He has already given the land to the people?

To answer the question, we go back to one of the premises of this book: mandate. Remember that God has relegated dominion over the world to mankind. In effect, God has given mankind free will almost right after the creation of the universe.

In *The General*, we explored how God gave Joshua a command to conquer Ai and gave him a picture of how to do it. It was Joshua who worked out the details of the plan to attack the city.

Moses had done the same for the twelve spies.

> Then Moses sent them to spy out the land of Canaan, and said to them, "Go up this way into the South, and go up to the mountains,

and see what the land is like: whether the people who dwell in it are strong or weak, few or many; whether the land they dwell in is good or bad; whether the cities they inhabit are like camps or strongholds; whether the land is rich or poor; and whether there are forests there or not. Be of good courage. And bring some of the fruit of the land." Now the time was the season of the first ripe grapes.

Numbers 13:17-20

After their reconnaissance mission, ten of the twelve spies cowered from what they saw in Canaan. Instead of coming up with a plan of attack with the information they had gathered, the prospect of facing giants and conquering walled cities got the best of them. Only Caleb and Joshua understood the assignment—they were the only ones who understood the objective. And because of that they were able to lay claim on God's promise.

"Will they fortify themselves?" Sanballat asked. "Will they complete it in a day? Will they revive the stones from the heaps of rubbish—stones that are burned?" The enemy was trying to sabotage their operation by undermining or questioning their objective. Had they let them, they would have ended up like ten of the twelve spies—unable to accomplish what they had set out to do.

Blur our purpose

An objective is something done to achieve a goal; purpose is the reason behind our actions that give them meaning. The objective is the "what." Purpose is the "why."

For the twelve spies, their objective was to spy out the land in order to make a strategy on how to conquer Canaan; their purpose was so that God's promise of an inheritance would be fulfilled through their obedience and faith in Him.

Nehemiah was part of a group of Jews who returned to Jerusalem, but theirs was not the first batch of returnees. They returned during the reign of King Artaxerxes around 445 BC. Almost a hundred years earlier, in about 540 BC, King Cyrus, the first Persian king to rule in Babylon, decreed that the Temple in Jerusalem be rebuilt.

> Now in the first year of Cyrus king of Persia [that is, the first year he ruled Babylon], in order to fulfill the word of the LORD by the mouth of Jeremiah [the prophet], the LORD stirred up (put in motion) the spirit of Cyrus king of Persia, so that he sent a proclamation throughout all his kingdom, and also put it in writing, saying: "Thus says Cyrus king of

Persia, 'The LORD, the God of heaven, has given me all the kingdoms of the earth and He has appointed me to build Him a house at Jerusalem, which is in Judah. Whoever there is among you of all His people, may his God be with him! Let him go up to Jerusalem, which is in Judah and rebuild the house of the LORD, the God of Israel; He is God who is in Jerusalem.

Ezra 1:1-3 AMP

Restoration would start two years after the return of the Israelites.

In the second year of their coming to God's house at Jerusalem, in the second month, Zerubbabel the son of Shealtiel and Jeshua the son of Jozadak began [the work], with the rest of their brothers—the priests and Levites and all who came to Jerusalem from the captivity. They appointed the Levites, from twenty years old and upward, to oversee the work of the house of the LORD. Then Jeshua with his sons and brothers stood united with Kadmiel and his sons, the sons of Judah and the sons of Henadad with their sons and brothers the Levites, to oversee the workmen in the house of God. Now when the builders had laid the foundation of the temple of the LORD, the priests stood in their apparel with trumpets, and the Levites, the sons of Asaph, with their cymbals, to praise the LORD in accordance with the directions of David king of Israel. They sang [responsively], praising and giving thanks to the LORD, saying, "For He is good, for His lovingkindness (mercy) toward Israel endures forever." And all the people shouted with a great shout when they praised the LORD because the foundation of the house of the LORD was laid.

Ezra 3:8-11 AMP

Their labor was far from smooth. They faced adversaries from all sides.

Then [the Samaritans and others of] the people of the land discouraged the people of Judah, and frightened them [to deter them] from building, and hired advisers [to work] against them to frustrate their plans during the entire time that Cyrus king of Persia reigned, [and this lasted] even until the reign of Darius king of Persia. Now in the reign of Ahasuerus (Xerxes), in the beginning of his reign, the Samaritans wrote [to him] an accusation against the inhabitants of Judah and Jerusalem [who had returned from exile]. Later, in the days of [King] Artaxerxes, Bishlam, Mithredath, Tabeel and the rest of their associates wrote to Artaxerxes king of Persia; and the text of the letter was written in Aramaic and translated from Aramaic.

Ezra 4:4-7 AMP

The "battle" raged on for several years until the original decree from King Cyrus was found and the reigning king fortified it.

And the Jewish elders built and prospered through the prophesying of Haggai the prophet and Zechariah the son of Iddo. They finished their building as commanded by the God of Israel and in accordance with the decree of Cyrus and Darius and Artaxerxes king of Persia. This temple was finished on the third day of the month of Adar, in the sixth year of the reign of King Darius.

Ezra 6:14-15 AMP

The Temple was finally rebuilt in about 516 BC—more than 20 years since the first batch returned. The first batch of ex-exiles returned to Jerusalem after about 70 years of exile in Babylon; Nehemiah, who would spearhead the rebuilding of the walls, returned after another 70 or so years since the Temple was rebuilt.

Before the Temple was rebuilt, they made offerings and sacrifices under distress.

> So they set up the altar on its [old] foundation, for they were terrified because of the peoples of the lands; and they offered burnt offerings on it to the LORD, morning and evening.
>
> Ezra 3:3 AMP

Enemy attacks may have somehow dwindled when the Persian king supported their work. But even then, the repercussions of having no wall around the city were deeper than physical harm. Without the wall, people from surrounding nations could just come and go unchecked. This resulted to intermarriages with the surrounding pagan people —something that the laws of Moses prohibited.

> When these things were completed, the officials came to me and said, "The people of Israel and the priests and Levites have not separated themselves from the peoples of the lands, but have committed the repulsive acts of the Canaanites, Hittites, Perizzites, Jebusites, Ammonites, Moabites, Egyptians, and Amorites. For they have taken some of their daughters as wives for themselves and for their sons, so that the holy race has intermingled with the peoples of the lands.

Indeed, the officials and chief men have been foremost in this unfaithful act and direct violation [of God's will]."

Ezra 9:1-2 AMP

Again, the broken down walls were just a picture of how broken and lost they were as a people.

The ex-exiles during the time of Nehemiah had the objective of rebuilding the walls. Their ultimate purpose was to give the people a venue where they can worship God without external threats—worship not just in terms of offering sacrifices but more importantly in how they conduct their lives.

Most of us might be able stop the enemy from denying our strength and from undermining our objective. But many lose focus on our ultimate purpose—which is to glorify God. It is very important that we recognize that we draw strength from God. It is equally important that we don't get worked up with the immensity of the work to be done to achieve our objectives. However, it is more important to never lose sight of our purpose.

THE FORTITUDE

In rebuilding the wall, the people were not just building fortifications. They were building their fortitude—their courage in the face of adversity.

It's clear that they had enemies around them trying to foil their efforts. But working as a team could present a challenge because they might end up building walls between each other.

Rebuilding the wall meant that they would need to work together as one. Working as one meant that they set their hearts on one objective. Setting their hearts on one thing meant getting rid of distractions and setting aside hindrances. It's like running a race as the writer of Hebrews would describe it centuries later.

> Therefore we also, since we are surrounded by so great a cloud of witnesses, let us lay aside every weight, and the sin which so easily ensnares us, and let us run with endurance the race that is set before us...
>
> Hebrews 12:1

It is quite important to lay aside these dead weights or else, we will be like the seed that fell among thorns in the Parable of the Sower.

> "Now these are the ones sown among thorns; they are the ones who hear the word, and the cares of this world, the deceitfulness of riches, and the desires for other things entering in choke the word, and it becomes unfruitful."
>
> Mark 4:18-19

"Will they fortify themselves?" Sanballat asked.

> So we built the wall, and the entire wall was joined together up to half its height, for the people had a mind to work.
>
> Nehemiah 4:6

Rebuilding the wall would not automatically rebuild the nation, but it's a start. However, rebuilding the wall to fortify the city was only half the work. Fortifying their sense of nationhood was equally important, if not more. And central to their sense of nationhood was their reverence to God who had chosen them to be His people.

With a rebuilt wall around the rebuilt Temple, they would then be able to worship God and diligently follow His law. God specifically told their forefathers to be strong and take courage—to have fortitude in the midst of adversities.

By obeying the command to be courageous and doing everything according to His law, the people allowed God to use them as instruments to further fulfill His promise to Abraham.

> "I will make you a great nation; I will bless you And make your name great; And you shall be a blessing."
>
> Genesis 12:2

THE VIGILANCE

The rebuilding of the wall was well on the way "for the people had a mind to work." But atrocities continued to hound the builders.

> Now it happened, when Sanballat, Tobiah, the Arabs, the Ammonites, and the Ashdodites heard that the walls of Jerusalem were being restored and the gaps were beginning to be closed, that they became very angry, and all of them conspired together to come and attack Jerusalem and create confusion.
>
> And our adversaries said, "They will neither know nor see anything, till we come into their midst and kill them and cause the work to cease."
>
> Nehemiah 4:7-8, 11

How did they respond?

> Nevertheless we made our prayer to our God, and because of them we set a watch against them day and night.
>
> Nehemiah 4:9

They prayed and watched.

Prayer is our first line of defense in spiritual battles.

Praying made perfect sense for the builders of the wall. When King Solomon dedicated the first Temple, God appeared before him and made one of the most powerful if-and-then statements in the Bible.

> "When I shut up heaven and there is no rain, or command the locusts to devour the land, or send pestilence among My people, if My people who are called by My name will humble themselves, and pray and seek My face, and turn from their wicked ways, then I will hear from heaven, and will forgive their sin and heal their land. Now My eyes will be open and My ears attentive to prayer made in this place."

> II Chronicles 7:13-15

It is sad that people almost always only do the "supplication" part of prayer—the part where we ask something from God. In the passage in II Chronicles 7, God spoke of a situation when blessings would be withheld from the people. This situation naturally would lead people to pray supplications. God basically laid down the steps to approach Him in prayer. "Pray" in the passage seems to mean "request." But it is only part of the formula that God provided.

The first part is for the people to humble themselves. To humble ourselves is to lower ourselves in the presence of someone of higher authority or power as a sign of reverence. When we humble ourselves before God, we acknowledge His sovereignty. This should be the first step when approaching the throne of God—before we lay down our requests. Requesting God for favors is absurd if we do not first acknowledge that He is sovereign over all and that it is well within His power to grant the desires of our hearts.

But it shouldn't stop there. God instructed the people to seek His face. To seek His face is to seek His approval—to come to Him in righteousness. But in *The Warrior*, where we discussed about the whole armor of God, we discovered that no one is righteous before God. In Old Testament times, when Jesus was not yet revealed, the law was the litmus paper for sin—for unrighteousness. When Jesus was revealed we learned that the law is not enough to make us righteous before God. Thus, we cannot approach Him with our own righteousness but only with the righteousness of Jesus.

> Obviously, the law applies to those to whom it was given, for its purpose is to keep people from having excuses, and to show that the entire world is guilty before God. For no one can ever be made right with God by doing what the law commands. The law simply

shows us how sinful we are. But now God has shown us a way to be made right with him without keeping the requirements of the law, as was promised in the writings of Moses and the prophets long ago. We are made right with God by placing our faith in Jesus Christ. And this is true for everyone who believes, no matter who we are.

Romans 3:19-22 NLT

And finally, humbling ourselves before God and seeking His face should result in turning from our wicked ways. Again, it is the result, not our ticket to God's favor and blessings.

In the verse from II Chronicles 7, "humble themselves," "pray," "seek My face," and "turn from their wicked ways" are stringed together with the conjunction "and." This simply means that all four actions should be present when we approach God. And the second part of God's statement was "then I will hear from heaven, and will forgive their sin and heal their land"—which was exactly the end result the builders were aiming for.

Nehemiah and the builders of the wall that would fortify the (second) Temple must have followed this formula when they prayed to God.

But prayer is simply recognizing that God will do His end of the bargain. So aside from praying to God, the people set a watch against the enemy day and night. This is the people holding their end of the bargain. Their endeavor required vigilance.

> Therefore I positioned men behind the lower parts of the wall, at the openings; and I set the people according to their families, with their swords, their spears, and their bows.
>
> And it happened, when our enemies heard that it was known to us, and that God had brought their plot to nothing, that all of us returned to the wall, everyone to his work. So it was, from that time on, that half of my servants worked at construction, while the other half held the spears, the shields, the bows, and wore armor; and the leaders were behind all the house of Judah. Those who built on the wall, and those who carried burdens, loaded themselves so that with one hand they worked at construction, and with the other held a weapon. Every one of the builders had his sword girded at his side as he built. And the one who sounded the trumpet was beside me.
>
> Nehemiah 4:13, 15-18

For Nehemiah and the builders, vigilance meant they had to defend themselves while working. Half of them worked while half of them stood guard. In addition, those who were working would work with one hand and carry a weapon in the other.

What does this mean for us, modern-day Christians? Again, we are in a constant battle with the enemy. The ex-exiles have shown us that for us to win every battle in this war, we must stay vigilant. In whatever we do, we have to have a weapon in one hand—the sword of the Spirit which is the Word of God.

Being in God's army, we are to equip ourselves with the Word.

> "This Book of the Law shall not depart from your mouth, but you shall meditate in it day and night, that you may observe to do according to all that is written in it. For then you will make your way prosperous, and then you will have good success."
>
> Joshua 1:8

Someone told me that we talk to God in our prayers and God talks to us through His written word—the Bible. This is what it means to be vigilant, especially in the present age.

The world bombards us everyday—especially in the advent of social media—with "wisdom." And the only way for us to really "fact check" or validate these tenets that the world presents us with is by comparing it to the truth in Scripture. The Holy Spirit in us, who is also called the Spirit of Truth, will guide us into all truth.

> "However, when He, **the Spirit of truth**, has come, He will guide you into all truth; for He will not speak on His own authority, but whatever He hears He will speak; and He will tell you things to come."
>
> John 16:13; emphasis mine

Remember that the Word of God is sharper than a double-edged sword. It is our ultimate weapon in this warfare.

> For the word of God is living and powerful, and sharper than any two-edged sword, piercing even to the division of soul and spirit, and of joints and marrow, and is a discerner of the thoughts and intents of the heart.
>
> Hebrews 4:12

Prayer and vigilance go together.

Knowing that we are in a war is acknowledging that there is an enemy who would do anything to deny our strength, undermine our objective, and blur our purpose. In order to win the war, we need fortitude and vigilance—especially in the spiritual realm.

EPILOGUE

The Great War is a-raging! Yet those on the side of truth, goodness, and life are assured of ultimate victory in the endgame—when our Champion, Jesus Christ, returns. When that time comes, our side will finally overcome the other. However, no one except the Father knows when.

> "But of that day and hour no one knows, not even the angels in heaven, nor the Son, but only the Father."
>
> Mark 13:32

Until then, the war is on. Again, there are only two sides; the war is binary. There is no middle ground. We should choose which side we are on. It's now or never. And I highly recommend we choose the side of truth and life.

When we confess that Jesus is Lord, we have already chosen a side. Let's suit up our armors and prepare to join the fray. We cannot sit idle while the war is waging. We cannot sit it out.

"Therefore whoever confesses Me before men, him I will also confess before My Father who is in heaven. But whoever denies Me before men, him I will also deny before My Father who is in heaven."

Matthew 10:32-33

Jesus, whose death and resurrection paved the way for the Holy Spirit to come, is our *anointing*.

Being Christlike is our compliance to the *rigors* of being children of God.

Our *mandate* emanates from Christ—to whom all authority has been given.

And all of *Scripture* points to Jesus—the Word who became flesh.

In Jesus, we are fully equipped with battle gears. There should be no room for fear to stand our ground.

We may be called to be in the vanguard if we want to help advance the Kingdom of God. We can do missions and go to the ends of the earth to reach out to the lost. This may not be for everyone but someone has to do it. It's a directive from Jesus Himself.

Everyone can be warriors. Warriors are those who are equipped for battle—anytime, anywhere. The Great War is fought on all fronts and on different levels. Warriors are those who have sufficient Biblical knowledge to stand fast in whatever circumstance. These battles can be as simple as conversations between friends or as structured as a formal debate. But warriors never back down—and everyone in the army should be a warrior in his or her own capacity.

The Great War is fought in the spiritual realm but it can manifest in the physical world. Conversely, what we do in the physical world can affect the spiritual realm. And our portal is prayer. We can be interceptors when we intercede in prayer. Praying—interceding—may be the least we can do that could have the greatest outcome.

No one ever said that Christians are not excel in endeavors other than advancing the Kingdom of God. We could and we should. Whenever we conquer new ground—in business or any endeavor—let's bring the name of Jesus. In everything we do, people should see Jesus in us. That's what it means to be a conqueror.

Those of us gifted with leadership skills can be generals in God's army—even in small ways. We could start a Bible study group and disciple the next generation of leaders. This is very important because any army must have someone taking the lead.

I believe many Christians are talented and skilled enough to do special operations to impact society. We could start a global movement, organize a conference, or write a book—anything which others can rally around to advance the Kingdom even further. That's being a special operative in the Army of God.

The Church—the Army of God—is a community of those of us who have put our faith in Jesus. As a community, we are to fortify each other as defense against the enemy. We are all builders of this community of faith—we are the engineering unit. And that community starts with the basic unit of society—the family.

Thus, we are all called to be men-at-arms—soldiers in the Army of God. The war may be far from over but we are assured of ultimate victory when Jesus returns!

> Then I turned to see the voice that spoke with me. And having turned I saw seven golden lampstands, and in the midst of the seven lampstands One like the Son of Man, clothed with a garment down to the feet and girded about the chest with a golden band. His head and hair were white like wool, as

white as snow, and His eyes like a flame of fire; His feet were like fine brass, as if refined in a furnace, and His voice as the sound of many waters; He had in His right hand seven stars, out of His mouth went a sharp two-edged sword, and His countenance was like the sun shining in its strength.

Revelation 1:12-16

Blessed is the man
Who walks not in the counsel of the
ungodly,
Nor stands in the path of sinners,
Nor sits in the seat of the scornful;
But his delight is in the law of the LORD,
And in His law he meditates day and
night.
He shall be like a tree
Planted by the rivers of water,
That brings forth its fruit in its season,
Whose leaf also shall not wither;
And whatever he does shall prosper.

Psalms 1:1-3

www.ingramcontent.com/pod-product-compliance
Lightning Source LLC
LaVergne TN
LVHW010513200726
843506LV00013B/2585